D0375157

OBALDIA

PLAYS VOLUME FOUR

OBALDIA

Monsieur Klebs and Rozalie
Translated by Barbara Wright

Wind in the Branches of the Sassafras
Translated by Joseph Foster

PLAYS VOLUME FOUR

JOHN CALDER : LONDON
RIVERRUN PRESS : NEW YORK

First published in Great Britain in 1985 by
John Calder (Publishers) Limited
18 Brewer Street London W1R 4AS
and in the USA by
Riverrun Press Inc
1170 Broadway, New York, NY 10001

Monsieur Klebs et Rozalie originally published in France
in 1975 by Editions Bernard Grasset.

Du vent dans les branches de sassafras originally
published in France in 1966 by Editions Bernard Grasset and
first published in Great Britain in 1969 by Calders & Boyars Ltd.

British Library Cataloguing in Publication Data
Obaldia, Réne de
    Plays.
    Vol. 4: Monsieur Klebs and Rozalie; Wind in
    the branches of the Sassafras.
    I. Title
    842'.914 PQ2629.B3

ISBN 0-7145-3664-4

SUBSIDISED BY THE
Arts Council
OF GREAT BRITAIN

Library of Congress Catalogue Number: 66-71262

Typeset in 9/10 point Times by Gilbert Composing Services,
Leighton Buzzard and printed in Great Britain by
Hillman Printers (Frome) Ltd, Frome, Somerset.

CHARACTERS

MONSIEUR KLEBS A scientist of intersidereal renown. Will he live to be fifty?

ROZALIE A computer. Klebs's creation, young and virginal—excessively feminine.

MADAME CHAFUT A force of nature—or, at any rate, a very strong-minded lady. Household duties. She guards Monsieur Klebs jealously; she thinks he's a nursery gardener.

DMITRY DMITRY-DMITRYOV A spy.

Monsieur Klebs et Rozalie was first performed on 15 September 1975 at the Théâtre de l'Oeuvre, directed by Jacques Rosny. The British premiere took place on 4 July 1980 at The Pitlochry Festival Theatre, directed by Vlado Habunek, with Andrew Melville as Monsieur Klebs and Kate Gielgud as Rozalie. American premiere, Spring 1985, at the Harold Clurman Theatre, New York.

MONSIEUR KLEBS AND ROZALIE

A Futurist Comedy

Preface

Monsieur Cordier, under the guise of an inoffensive nursery gardener living in a small village, is, in fact, the famous Doctor Klebs, 'a scientist of intersidereal renown, the genius of the century, the man of parallel equations', as he ironically defines himself.

The custodian of terrifying secrets, he has managed to escape the great powers for whom he used to work, and who spent fortunes competing for his services. He is no longer willing for the results of his labour to fall into the hands of the politicians or the military. For a dozen years, constantly moving from country to country and changing his identity, he has managed to put people off the scent: they believe him to be dead. (With the possible exception of a certain Dmitry Dmitry-Dmitryov . . .). As soon as he has finished playing at being a gardener, 'Monsieur Cordier' continues his researches in a converted basement adjoining the house he has rented.

It is here that we discover him, as the curtain rises, plunged in his calculations and conversing with a machine that resembles a computer: Rozalie. A strange machine, that seems to be made out of odds and ends—a wood and metal framework with pipes and bellows—out of the top part of which, in the semi-darkness, emerges a woman's face. Is a woman imprisoned in this matrix, or is she an integral part of the machine? However this may be, 'Rozalie', who abounds in femininity and is also in possession of a colossal amount of knowledge (she has absorbed hundreds of magnetic tapes), converses, argues or jokes with her creator. (Her one defect, though it will be seen to be fraught with consequences, is that, at certain moments, she lisps.) And between Ivan Klebs and the machine, a cold, extraordinary love story will unfold.

With her, the scientist dreams of begetting a new humanity in which 'man will behave like a man to his fellow men'. But the espionage department will catch up with him. Monsieur Klebs will fail in his Faustian undertaking. His creation, too, will have been but a dream . . .

Note: This succinct résumé, intended for the press, and possibly for the programme—the public is ever avid to know in advance what sort of food it's going to have to digest—has the advantage of talking adroitly about the play without giving away any of its essentials.

Notes for production

It is important that, right from his first entry, Monsieur Klebs should be presented to us as a familiar, everyday character.

The strangeness of the situation, the immensity of his knowledge and his dialogue with the machine must seem entirely natural. His obvious contempt for inessentials and the comic side of his absent-mindedness become apparent when he goes to look for his tin of coffee in a hat box, for instance, or when, mulling over his interior equations, he puts his slipper on his head instead of his hat when he's about to go out. If we wanted to take a great scientist as a model, it's Einstein we would think of: humanity, simplicity, even gaiety, in spite of an acute awareness of living in apocalyptic times.

Monsieur Klebs's extremism should only gradually become noticeable.

At the beginning of the play, Rozalie should speak in a mechanical voice. As it proceeds, however, she may change her register, modulate, and surprise even her creator by her ironic or sensual inflections, as if she were making fun of herself.

In the second act, when she becomes a woman and exerts her powers of seduction, she must remember to make certain automatic movements to remind us of the machine that she also is: her attitude , walk, sudden mechanical gestures, the way she connects herself to a power point to recover her strength, etc. These automatic moments will be brief, but they will be enough to remind the audience of Rozalie's double nature.

Finally: the character of Rozalie as created by Annie Sinigalia gave the impression of a young woman in possession of the subtle, obscure and inexhaustible resources of a pseudo-daughter of Eve. It is also conceivable that the part might be played by a 'child-woman', whose age might be anything between thirteen and fifteen.

ACT I

The room in which MONSIEUR KLEBS *has taken refuge, in order to devote himself to his labours in secret.*

It's a basement room, a sort of cellar with a glass roof which lets the daylight in. (It is summer).

A staircase leads up to a door to the outside; it is opened from below, by pulling on a rope.

Inside, fantastic disorder. A table cluttered with books, papers, magazines, scientific instruments. A dustbin overflowing with the remains of magnetic tapes. A bicycle wheel. Trunks, cardboard boxes, a rocking chair. On a packing case, a camping stove, on which is enthroned a coffee pot. Plants. A bowl hanging from the ceiling, in which two goldfish are chasing each other. Socks drying on a line.

In a corner of the room, more or less concealed, a computer: ROZALIE.

A strange computer. It seems to be made out of odds and ends–a wood and metal framework with pipes, bellows, a vegetable shredder–out of the top part of which will emerge, whenever it pleases KLEBS, *a woman's face. Is* ROZALIE *imprisoned in this matrix, or is she an integral part of the machine. Blackboard, on which is clearly chalked up:* $E + I = MC^3$.)

Scene One

M. KLEBS, ROZALIE

The stage is empty for a few seconds. Then the door to the outside opens and MONSIEUR KLEBS *appears. He is dressed as a gardener (straw hat, apron fastened round his waist, thick gloves). He is carrying an enormous plant whose leaves partly hide his face. He comes cautiously down the stairs, puts the plant down in a corner, takes from his apron pocket a pair of secateurs, a screwdriver, and a little saw which he hangs on the wall with a routine gesture. He chucks his hat into a corner, pulls off his gloves, sits down in the armchair and takes off his shoes, whilst pursuing his thoughts.*

KLEBS *(putting on a slipper)*.   We can't say that things are getting any better.
ROZALIE *(neutral voice)*.   We certainly can't.
Slight pause.
KLEBS.   And yet, some people maintain . . . Utopians! Mongols! . . . Personally—and my person is of enormous value—personally, I say that we can't say.

ROZALIE.   Can't say.
KLEBS.   Nicht.
ROZALIE.   Nicht.
KLEBS.   Niet.
ROZALIE.   Niet.

Klebs stands up, goes over to the machine and, while tightening some obscure screws:

KLEBS.   In fact, things never have got better. From the very beginning, the blood of massacres has continued to circulate; an uninterrupted river: the blood of innocents. Ever since there has been strife on this planet . . .
ROZALIE *(correcting him).*   Ever since there has been **life** on this planet.
KLEBS.   Ever since there has been life on this planet, ever since the protozoa, the sea urchin, the one-legged cell; ever since the Negus, the diplodocus, diplomacy, nothing has ever really worked. Man still behaves like a wolf to his fellow men.
ROZALIE *(sententiously).*   Man: vertical insolence.
KLEBS.   And religions, all the religions that preach love, humility, the washing of feet, they haven't in any way modified his behaviour. They've never managed to reduce the arrogance of the deplorable upstart. All religion including the one true one . . . *(He turns a little handle at the corner of the machine: we see* ROZALIE'S *head emerge. Then, pursuing his operations in the guts of the machine.)* The son of God, so obstinately Jewish, has acquired such a taste for martyrdom that, even quite recently, he volunteered for Auschwitz, Buchenwald, Dachau, Treblinka, with all his disciples: six million star-spangled subjects! Enough to make you vomit. To make you despair.
ROZALIE *(energetically).*   No no, Monsieur Klebs, you mustn't despair. You are 'Monsieur Klebs'. Remember that you are 'Monsieur Klebs'. Have faith in Klebs! The least of your cells dies and is reborn calling out: Klebs! Klebs! Klebs! Klebs! Klebs! Klebs!
KLEBS *(irritated).*   That's enough of that record, Rozalie; you're getting on my nerves.
ROZALIE *(entreating him).*   Don't talk to me in that metallic voice, Monsieur Klebs, you're hurting my electromagnetic unit.
KLEBS.   **Now** what are you going on about?
ROZALIE.   You know very well, Monsieur Klebs, that I've been ill. Overloading! Overloading! Pressure on the thalamus and disturbance of the cortex! And that you have to treat me gently. *(Coquettishly)* Or better still—do me a favour . . . *(Slight pause)* Do me a favour, Monsieur Klebs; tell me who you are?
KLEBS.   Again!
ROZALIE.   Yes, again! Every time you give me your coordinates it recharges me, it gives me some extra neutrons, a whole flux of neutrons . . . When you nourish me with your destiny, I increase my jubilationary potential. Bitte schön! Once again! Who are you, Monsieur Klebs?
KLEBS *(goes over to the stove on the packing case and lights it, intending to make himself a cup of coffee. As if reciting a lesson learnt by heart).*   Klebs.

Ivan Klebs. Scientist of intersidereal renown. The brain of the century. The man of parallel equations.

ROZALIE (*with relish*)   The man of parallel equations.

KLEBS.   A vast mental organisation . . . I have worked in the secret laboratories and factories of the great powers. I have done research with Oppenheimer, Andreïv, Strogonoff, von Braun, Akäi-Kakito, Browning and Barclay, Lavastine, Bröjstrom, forever moving from one enemy to the next . . . Which is why the counter-espionage departments could never arrest me: whenever they managed to catch up with me, I was already working for the country that was employing them . . . (*A laugh from the machine, a sound like a rusty weathercock revolving in the wind*). When I had sufficiently decorticated the atom, when I'd left anti-matter without a leg to stand on and it had become established beyond doubt that none of them had any more to teach me, I escaped . . . A great big gap, all of a sudden, in the scientific sky! And also—panic!—I was in possession of some formidable secrets. The order went out to find me at all costs, and if necessary—to kill me! . . . For a long time they searched for me in Nepal, in Siberia, in North Berlin, in Israel, in Buenos Aires, in Conflans-Sainte-Honorine, in the Canary Islands . . .

ROZALIE.   What a lot of travelling I made you do, Monsieur Klebs!

KLEBS (*drinking his coffee*).   It was on a barge I'd hired at Conflans that I really conceived you, Rozalie.

ROZALIE.   Oh! Really! On a barge!

KLEBS.   After a desperate, gruelling struggle, all of a sudden—the formula! The magic formula that descends upon you like grace. Eureka! . . . While I was watching a cigarette butt being carried away by the current.

ROZALIE.   A classic story, Monsieur Klebs. I must already have recorded that somewhere.

KLEBS (*to himself, his suppressed anger suddenly showing*).   Eureka! And yet, even now, there's still something that escapes me, something of primary importance . . . I'm stuck! I'm stuck!

ROZALIE.   And after that, Monseiur Klebs? After Eureka?

KLEBS (*coming back to Rozalie*).   The Canary Islands, Lausanne, Hong Kong, Panama; I managed to put them off the scent. For the last twelve years they've believed me to be dead. Except, perhaps, Dmitry Dmitry-Dmitryov . . . Some people maintain that my corpse is in a cement vessel containing atomic waste at the bottom of the Pacific.

ROZALIE.   You'll certainly end by exploding, Monsieur Klebs!

KLEBS.   Oh really, Rozalie, you might spare me your stupid jokes. (*A frightful squawk from the machine*). And don't squawk like that, it's not decent. (*A pause*). In fact, if you really want to grasp my . . .

ROZALIE (*eagerly*).   Oh yes!

KLEBS *is surprised by* ROZALIE's *tone*.

KLEBS.   If you really want to grasp my meaning, you must understand that I have a profound knowledge of all the sciences: geophysics, biochemistry, astronomy, neurology, sexology, and all the latest 'ologies', 'ics' and so on: genetics, electronics, data processing, problematics, wave mechanics, to mention only a few. On these grounds I might well be considered to be . . . to be . . .

ROZALIE. To be the first globalist.

KLEBS. To be the first globalist. As a general rule, it is to be observed that every specialist specialises in his own speciality. **My** idea was to specialise in **all** the specialities. Hence my fabulous range, my approach to the universal . . . It's simple, but **someone** had to think of it. If all the specialists were to abandon their specialities for those of other people, we might well see a cardiologist, for instance, becoming the master of Prometheus's liver, and shutting his eagle up in a jar of surgical spirit!

ROZALIE. Oh là là!

KLEBS. What's the matter, Rozalie?

ROZALIE. Nothing, Monsieur Klebs, nothing.

KLEBS. Obviously, memorisation of this sort on a cosmic scale is not without its dangers. I was locked up for eighteen months in a psychiatric hospital in Dyhernfurth, in Germany. Looked after by Soviet nurses who spoke Portuguese to put people off the scent, and treated by pseudo-doctors whose faces changed every time they leant over mine . . . Not to mention the miniature mikes they put into my stomach; my abdomen became a miniature listening console . . . But I always remained lucid, thanks to my training in the psychic depths. It was only the surface that was off the rails. Under the influence of certain drugs, I revealed secrets that weren't secrets at all, and I invented ad lib formulas for overpowering the developed countries—formulas which were reported to various statesmen, the result being a further obfuscation of their intelligence—which was already pretty lamentable.

ROZALIE. Liming the twig for the little birdies, eh! . . . And then what, Monsieur Klebs? Then what?

KLEBS. Then I shut myself up in my ivory blockhaus. Walking round and round like a lion or a tiger in the cage of my nuptial spirit. With one hand, doling out peanuts to the monkeys of the night; with the other, shoving the face of my guardian angel into a bath of quick lime. And great expanses of darkness would disappear, revealing jittery old men; cocks with their heads cut off ran amok in a panic of feathers, searching for their cries of anguish. And the dawn knocked at my armour-plated door, and whenever I opened it, I found myself face to face with a little girl, who was purple, and blind.

ROZALIE. You're becoming literary, Monsieur Klebs . . . And then what? . . . And then? (KLEBS *maintains an obstinate silence*). . . . All those years of study, of solitude; all those nights wounded by the crowing of blind cocks; all your incoherent, extravagant science; your orphaned formulas, your uterine equations . . . all leading to what? (*Sensually*) . . . leading to what?

KLEBS (*suddenly falling on his knees in front of the machine and embracing it amorously*). Leading to you, Rozalie! To you, to you, my goddess! To you, my deaconess! To you! To you!

ROZALIE (*embarrassed*). Oh come, Monsieur Klebs, get up! Please get up!

KLEBS. To you, my quivering, squeaking, leaping, glittering . . .

ROZALIE. No, really, behave yourself! At your age! (*Blushing, as if he had been fondling her*) Monsieur, Monsieur, Monsieur Klebs!

KLEBS (*standing up just as abruptly as he had fallen on his knees, brushing his trousers with his hand, walking up and down*). A momentary weakness; take no notice, Rozalie, it's only human . . . Can you understand that a creator can be made delirious by his creation? That his greatest temptation can be to lose himself in her? We have even seen gods abandoning Olympus and turning themselves into eagles, bulls, swans, earthworms, in order to penetrate the innermost recesses of their make-up. As if they were seeking the secret of their own secret . . . Yes, it's delirium. You make me delirious, Rozalie.

ROZALIE. Don't make me blush, Monsieur Klebs.

KLEBS. Compared with you, Rozalie, the human beings I come into contact with seem insipid—interchangeable. The same motivation. The same mechanism. Petty lives with petty problems. Petty lives, petty deaths. Ghosts! Zombies! Thousands of sociologists! In the year 2000—brace yourself, Rozalie—in the year 2000, they anticipate that there will be seven thousand million people on our planet. Seven thousand million ghosts. Seven thousand million robots.

ROZALIE. Robots who'll be hungry.

KLEBS. Yes, seven thousand million alimentary canals.

KLEBS *goes over to the goldfish bowl. Picking up a pipette, he dips it into the bowl and sucks up the water. Having quenched his thirst:*

KLEBS. Water full of phosphorus! . . . Genius makes you thirsty. Thirsty for phosphorus. Thirsty for sidereal tears. (*talking to the fish.*) Little goldfish, little red goldfish, my little plumbers, my little rockets, my little cardinals, my moist . . . High and dry, and yet still moist! (*To himself.*) Any minute now, what with the progress of science, all the red goldfish will be greenish, verdigris, and they won't have any more bones, and they won't need to swim . . . (*To the fish.*) And they'll never, never wet their beds! (*A pause.*) All the same, I really would have liked to be the pope.

ROZALIE. The pope!

KLEBS. A worker pope . . . A managing director pope . . . A trade unionist pope. A plastic-bombed pope: pssht! shot up to heaven, and butting his head into the Trinity!

   The pope.

   God's representative on earth.

   'No representatives allowed in this building' . . . The pope, the last pope, a door-to-door salesman, suitcase in hand: 'Can I interest you in a little bit of eternity, lady?'

   The 'lady' pushes him out: 'What if my husband saw us!'

ROZALIE. I know you've had very little sleep the last few nights, Monsieur Klebs.

KLEBS. To put myself in the pope's shoes; to short-circuit the Holy Ghost. No—to **be** the Holy Ghost. (*Radiantly*). **I am** the Holy Ghost, Rozalie, I speak all the languages of the earth, I lick all my brides with a little tongue of fire. Intrepidity, come to my aid! I commute between the Father and the Son, sitting in my cybernetic nacelle, drawn by doves with their magnetic fuselage, with their apostolic eye . . .

ROZALIE.   Apostolic eye.

KLEBS.   And here I am, before the throne of the Father.

Father, I bring you this missive from Your Son . . . And it's always the same love letter, the same fiery letter. Which is why the sun still rises in the east.

ROZALIE (*as if to a child*).   Monsieur Klebs, you . . .

KLEBS.   And the Father laughs up the sleeve of his nightgown, and gives me back the Son's missive to take back to the Son. Off you go, doves!

Your Son, I bring you this missive from Our Father.

And the Son hasn't waited for my words; he takes the missive out of my mouth, and the loving words transfix him, and the blood flows from his flanks . . . Which is why the sun still sets in the west.

ROZALIE.   Monsieur Klebs, you ought to have a rest, filter your fumes, air-condition your overheating . . .

KLEBS.   A rest! **You** tell me I ought to rest! When I'm stuck, I'm stuck, and you make me . . . (*Slight pause. Pulling himself together, and speaking in a soapy tone of voice which is intended to be conciliatory.*) Rozalie, I'm going to try once again to explain to you . . . (*Taking a deep breath.*) Rozalie . . .

ROZALIE (*very humbly*).   Yes, Monsieur Klebs.

KLEBS.   Rozalie, I have made you the heiress to my genius, to my genius raised by its own genetical law to the ninth power, and embellished by Coulomb's law, which I will now venture to recall to your memory. (*He goes to the blackboard on which he writes the formula as he states it. Oddly enough, at the end of his demonstration, the figures and segments he has chalked up have turned into a human head.*) Each corpuscle is associated with a constant charge, either positive, negative or zero, which is called the 'Electric Charge of the Corpuscle.' E.C.C.

ROZALIE.   Yes, Monsieur Klebs.

KLEBS.   Therefore, between two corpuscles, C_1 and C_2, charged with charges E_1 and E_2, a force called an 'electrostatic force' is exerted, whose intensity is in direct proportion to the charges, and in inverse proportion to the square of the distance between the points representing the aforementioned corpuscles . . . An electrostatic force from which you benefit without the slightest restriction.

ROZALIE.   Yes, Monsieur Klebs.

KLEBS.   I have endowed you with the longest possible memory: you can recite by heart, and in no matter what order, 'Don Quixote', Saint Thomas Aquinas, 'Romeo and Juliet', 'The Thousand and One Nights', Clausewitz, Schaeffer, Maine de Biran, The Marquis de Sade, Kotzebue, Kafka, 'The Talmud', 'The Divine Comedy', the romantic poets, etc., etc. In short, every kind of invigorating and soothing literature, all the philosophical treatises, all the historical textbooks, all the Encyclopaedias, all the incalculable knowledge of all possible ignoramuses, and even the entire contents of Libraries that have been reduced to dust . . .

ROZALIE.   Yes, Monsieur Klebs.

KLEBS. You can solve the trickiest problems in the twinkling of an eye. You can compose random and totally inexplicable poems, write contraceptive music . . . You have managed to psychoanalyse Freud, to make Marx and all the prophets bald, to scramble the Listening Consoles of the Law on Mount Sinai . . . You are capable of grazing on silence, and of digesting it.

ROZALIE. Yes, Monsieur Klebs.

KLEBS. Thanks to the Law of Large Numbers, which I have perfected by means of the Law of Small Numbers, you can read the thoughts of anyone who happens to be in your presence . . . Your telepathic powers even extend so far as to pick up the thoughts of people who have been dead for centuries, to recapitulate whole sentences dispersed in time and space . . . The extreme mobility of your sensory nucleo-compartmentalised mechanisms makes it possible for you to carry on a conversation with any kind of scientist, and also with any kind of village idiot.

ROZALIE. Oh yes, Monsieur Klebs.

KLEBS (*furious*). Oh yes, Monsieur Klebs! Oh yes, Monsieur Klebs! . . . Well then, will you kindly explain why, contrary to all the accepted rules, and without the slightest warning, you suddenly start to lisp? (*a painful silence*.) Will you kindly tell me why?

ROZALIE. . . .

KLEBS. For months and months I've been stuck, just because of that ridiculous detail! You lisp—you lithp!—you sound like a half-witted finishing-school female! (*Imitating her*.) 'If it ithn't putting you to too much twouble, I'd love another gwapefuit juithe, with a little gin—jutht a dwop!' . . . And when you lisp—and this is where it becomes tragic—it's a sure sign that all your senses have gone haywire, that your fundamental particles have got debauched. You lisp, and then you go off the rails; you pick the wrong tape or you play it at the wrong speed . . . Don't you remember?—three days ago, I asked you a question about Heisenberg's Uncertainty Principle, and you answered: 'Gather ye Rose-buds while ye may.' . . . My blood froze. I banged my head against my knees for a whole hour. I can't sleep any more. All my science reduced to a skeleton. A fault that can't even be attributed to heredity! You're a virgin, Rozalie! You are the most virginal of all virgins!

ROZALIE. Yes, Monsieur Klebs.

KLEBS. Yes, Monsieur Klebs—that's all you can say! All my Problematics of the Absolute chucked away in a single second! . . . After all the sacrifices I've made for you! All the anti-matter lessons I've given you! The ecumenical principles I've inculcated into you! The evenings when I might have gone to the cinema, or to the strip-tease . . . No, Mademoiselle lisps! Mademoiselle insists on lisping! And on losing her particles, and on giving herself liquid airs! Why not unlearn everything, then? Why not simply erase the tapes and play cards? (*Silence*.) And as always, when I ask you this question, your lips are sealed. You look down your nose and let me go on talking and talking . . . I simply can't understand; I keep losing myself in conjecture. (*He buries his nose in a big exercise book covered with equations*). Maybe I need to know more about matrix calculus? . . . Or else . . . Or else . . . (*Shutting his exercise book: affably.*) Tell me, Rozalie, when you suddenly start to lisp, does it have anything to do with your sense of humour? Does it? I ask you in all humility . . . Humour, by its very nature, plays leap-frog over the back of all equations; leap-frog. Maybe, quite unintentionally, a mysterious combination of exponential relations has caused an overflow, a superabundance, in your mechanism?—to be precise, a touch of humour—which you translate into those series of soft sibilants? Could this phenomenon be your way of inflating your tubes? (*Furious.*) Or could it be, quite simply, that you're taking the piss out of me? (*Pause.*) Anyway, that's quite enough talk with you. (*He turns the handle;* ROZALIE'S *head disappears into the machine.*) I've been spoiling you, my beauty, I've been spoiling you! My conversation may well provide you with a few extra neutrons, but personally I'm suffering from a loss of psychic energy, with humoral disorders. A luxury I can't afford. Lisp in your wires, if you like, or chew over the properties of wave function, I wash my hands of the whole business! Much too good. Much too decent. Much too . . . (*He disconnects some wires. An indicator light goes out.*) Phew! Alone at last! (*He goes back to his work table and throws some papers covered with equations into the waste paper basket.*) Homo solus aut deus, aut daemon, as Juvenal said. Which we may translate as: A man alone is either a saint or a . . . or a Juvenal delinquent! (*He laughs like mad at his ghastly pun, rushes over to the machine and reconnects its wires.*) That's the best ever! Did you hear that, Rozalie? Either a saint or a Juvenal delinquent! (*Scornful silence from* ROZALIE. KLEBS *disconnects her again, offended.*) Right.

KLEBS *goes over to the blackboard, rubs out the equation* $E + I = MC^3$, *and writes feverishly:*

$$20x + 5y \quad 2z = 24$$
$$3x + 10y \quad 4z = 11$$

Turning round to the audience.

I was a sickly child, temperamental, epidermal . . . But with very beautiful blue eyes . . . Unique—an only child. (*At the blackboard*)

$$x + 2y + 3z = 95$$
$$x = 1.2$$
$$y = 1.1$$

To the audience.

I suffered a great deal through not having a little sister, through not being able to pull her pigtails . . . My mother used to ask me: Why don't you ever smile? Why don't you play with your little friends? Why do you lock yourself in the lavatory for hours on end? . . . My father finally stopped talking to me altogether. (*At the blackboard, and as if there were a cause and effect relationship*) Therefore:

$$z = 3.17$$

Feverishly

To get to the point where all this simulation would culminate in the absolute truth. (*Puts down his chalk and once again paces up and down the room.*) My poor parents! My insoluble progenitors! ... One evening, at the end of her tether, my mother exclaimed: I must have sinned against the good Lord for him to send me a child like you. What can have got into me? And I answered—I must have been seven years old—: Me, mother! Another evening—before the mere sight of me struck him dumb, my father yelled at me: You're always there but you're never there! You look right through me as if I were a window pane! No but really, who d'you think you are? ... And I answered: I'm X, Papa; I think I'm X, the unknown. The unknown, an unknown factor, a factor of glory and cataclysms, Papa!

Obviously this way of speaking was a bit above him. But it wasn't my fault that hereditary intelligence had skipped a few generations so as to become concentrated in my cerebral cortex. Whereas he, the dear old fellow, apart from fucking ... A greater fucker, we must give him credit for that. The number of women who succumbed to the capital letter of his nothingness! In the end my mother, in view of the extent of his ravages, the oceans of multiplied wombs, went so far as to doubt that I had ever come out of **her** womb. She clasped me to her bosom, she panted ... And I, in this scene—all I could show was logistic ingratitude. I sincerely pity the womb that is delivered a genius. (*He goes back to the blackboard and checks his calculations.*) To cram all the complexity of the universe into a thimble. Every achievement is repressive. Weeding. Pruning. Suppressing, suppressing, suppressing! (*Going over to* ROZALIE.) I shall eventually reduce this machine to a scream, and make it produce—Rozalie. (*Banging his fist on the machine.*) There's a woman in there! (*Coming back upstage.*) Delirium! Delirium! Who could possibly understand the vacillation of the mind, when the mind can no longer distinguish the frontier between its own identity and that of matter, and when matter itself takes it into its head to start thinking? ... That's when we turn to the goldfish. Little goldfish, little goldfish ... We read the daily papers from cover to cover, we run our fingers over the furniture to see whether it's been properly dusted, we come back to ordinary, decent, puerile society:—'Lovely day isn't it, Madame Chafut, lovely; but it won't last!' ... So as not to go mad, we take refuge in the obvious—the so-called obvious ... (*A pause. Then, somewhat wearily.*) There are moments when I feel like falling on my knees and appealing to the god of Pythagoras, of Virgil, of Einstein; to the god of mutations and permutations, to the Eternal Lord; yes, on my knees!—don't let's be afraid of being ridiculous. (*He falls on his knees in front of the packing case with the camping stove on it.*) There! ... 'Monsieur Kleb's prayer to the Eternal Lord':

O Lord, make the earth to be round like a globe!

Let Thy centrifugal force, zero at the Poles, and maximal at the Equator, make it also slightly flattened towards those Poles, and thus approximate to an oblate spheroid in shape which revolves in elliptical orbits about the sun.

Engendering the calends and the ides,
And blessed be this fluid mass!

****

O Lord, make the azure to be blue, make the grass to be green, let
wrath be red, let oranges be orange, let bishops be violet,
O Lord, let what is bred in the bone come out in the flesh,
And let the spirit be more and more willing.
Let the kid call to the kid,
The rose to the rosemary,
Let the hart spring from the heart
And blessed be the turtle-dove!

****

Let the peacock spread its tail
And the tale spread its peacock
Let the apple be an apple
And fall on Newton,
Let the wind for evermore have cherubs' hands,
Hands to tuck up the skirts of all lands,
And blessed be the petticoats of blessed damozels!

****

O Lord, give us this day our daily
Animal,
Vegetable,
And Mineral,
And deliver us from . . . Man!

****

Protect our humus
And our Rhesus
Factor,
And bless the custard of Pi R squared.
O Lord, make the rainbow to be eternally curved,
And preserve the bear, that honey may be preserved.

****

And pour Thine eternity and thy love
Into the breath of the new-born,
Into the breath of the firmament above,
Into those entering the developing country of the dead,
And into the sunflower, and into the red
Cyclamen,
And into the song of the first swallow of summer,
And let Rozalie and me never have any children.
Amen!

KLEBS *stands up.*

Yes, I have reached this fundamental concept, this conclusion—which is both optimistic and desperate—desperately optimistic: it couldn't have been done better! Congratulations! A fabulous piece of machinery A hurly-burly of genius; nothing but functional equations. Congratulations! All reverence to your Reverence. What would it have been like if . . . For after all, things aren't getting any better! The worst is becoming more and more inevitable.

Knocks at the door. KLEBS *hurriedly covers up the machine. Then he pulls the rope: the door opens. Enter* MADAME CHAFUT.

Scene II

KLEBS, ROZALIE, MADAME CHAFUT

KLEBS (*relieved*).   Ah! It's you, Madame Chafut.
MME CHAFUT (*coming down the stairs*).   Well, Monsieur Cordier?
KLEBS.   Well, Madame Chafut? Well?
MME CHAFUT.   Always muttering to yourself down there. And what about your stew?
KLEBS.   What about my stew?
MME CHAFUT.   Your stew's getting cold, Monsieur Cordier!
KLEBS (*looking at his watch*).   Ten past twelve! My stew may well be getting cold, but I have already asked you, Madame Chafut, not to barge in like that, like a bulldozer, without warning, into my laboratory. It's most annoying; you know very well that my inspiration doesn't come easily, that I'm very highly-strung . . .
MME CHAFUT.   Doesn't surprise me. Always shut up in your basement like a mole! If I didn't force my way in from time to time it's a safe bet that one day I'd find a mummy! You can't call this a life! A man like you, in the prime of his blood, a fine figure of a man, well-endowed, virile, and so on. And even if you are highly-strung . . .
KLEBS.   Listen, Madame Chafut, I appreciate your solicitude . . .
MME CHAFUT.   I like music, too: 'Madam Butterfly', 'Louise', 'The Pearl Fishers' . . . It doesn't follow! Well then, how far've you got with your futurist symphony?
KLEBS.   Oh, I still have a long way to go.
MME CHAFUT (*pointing to* ROZALIE).   And you make it all up with your machine there?
KLEBS.   I've already explained it to you, Madame Chafut. Thanks to that machine, in fact, I record on magnetic tape, I . . .
MME CHAFUT.   You record **what**, exactly? Draughts? No one ever comes down into your cellar. Not even a cat!
KLEBS.   I plug it into the radio, or I use records. I record voices, sighs, retransmissions of football matches, fragments of 'Madam Butterfly', silences, explosions . . . draughts! Then I select, I compose, I superimpose, I decompose, I mix.

MME CHAFUT.   The work of a maniac, with all due respect. Ah well, we all have our hobbies. Mine's baby clothes; I can't help it, I just have to knit for all the new-born babies of the universe! But even so, Monsieur Cordier, you ought to get a bit of fresh air, not always stay down here in your cellar, like a mushroom.

KLEBS.   A mole, a mummy, a mushroom! What next?

MME CHAFUT.   Don't be offended, Monsieur Cordier, it was only a suggestion . . . But I'm not the only one in the village who thinks that . . . Monsieur Eon, for instance . . . Ah yes, Monsieur Eon!

KLEBS.   What about Monsieur Eon?

MME CHAFUT.   The gutter that came pissing down on him last night, in the kitchen. The plumber can't be bothered to put himself out for at least a month. So he asked me if you could possibly go round . . . Oh yes, and there's Mademoiselle Mauduit, too, now I come to think of it.

KLEBS.   The new schoolmistress?

MME CHAFUT.   Yes, Mademoiselle Mauduit. She got a short-circuit in her hands with her washing machine. I found her trembling all over, like a sheet. I thought only Monsieur Cordier would come and see me, she kept babbling.

KLEBS.   Monsieur Eon, Mademoiselle Mauduit: The day before yesterday it was Madame Pierret. Madame Pierret's bladder. 'My bladder's flared up, Monsieur Cordier, it feels as if it's on fire down there.' 'Cherry stalks, Madame Pierret, cherry stalks; my regards to Monsieur Pierret!' A week ago it was the curé.

MME CHAFUT.   The curé, in any case, no one'd ever know he **was** a curé. Always running around in his underpants, with the junior team.

KLEBS.   I'm perfectly willing to do favours for people from time to time, but there's a difference between that and people taking me for . . . for I don't know what!

MME CHAFUT.   It's always the same: you give your little finger and they take the whole works! You know what I think, Monsieur Cordier? . . . Being as how you're such a jack of all trades, if you had your wits about you you'd become a specialist.

KLEBS.   A specialist?

MME CHAFUT.   A plumber, for instance. Plumbing would be more of a paying proposition than your nursery gardening. These days, plumbers simply rake it in—for a start, what about their travelling expenses? You only have to cross the road, and you hand in your bill!

KLEBS.   Thank you for your advice, Madame Chafut. My trade, that of nursery gardener, may not pay me as well as plumbing would, but it does allow me some leisure—I have time to spare for my hobbies, for my sonic research.

MME CHAFUT.   All right, all right; it was only a suggestion . . . And anyway, if everyone went in for Christmas trees, or old-time dancing, there'd certainly be less misery in the world. We can't say that things are getting any better.

KLEBS.   Hm! We certainly can't.

MME CHAFUT.   Did you hear this morning, on the radio? Three terrorists have hijacked a Japanese plane: they're Swiss. They're fed up with being Swiss, that's what they told the authorities at Djibouti. Yes, they're grounded at Djibouti for the moment. 160° in the shade in the fuselage. And not a single ounce of air left to condition. And they want to be refuelled by six air hostesses wearing the miniest of all mini costumes. And all the passengers are in danger of dying of thirst. In my day, maybe it wasn't Eldorado, but we did exist. Didn't need to kill people just to get in the news. Hm! . . . Speaking of Eldorado, wasn't that in Peru?

KLEBS. It could have been.

MME CHAFUT. And Lima, that's in Peru too, isn't it?

KLEBS. Yes; Lima is in Peru.

MME CHAFUT. Well, a general there has just had twelve others shot— twelve other generals. At that rate the Indians'll have to look after themselves, there'll be no one left to defend them!

KLEBS. And what about my stew, Madame Chafut?

MME CHAFUT. Your stew? My goodness me, your stew! It'll be yesterday's left-overs at this rate. Come on up, Monsieur Cordier; while I'm heating it up we can have a chat.

KLEBS. You go ahead, Madam Chafut; I'll be with you in three minutes— that'll give me time to put all these papers away.

MME CHAFUT (*going up the stairs*). There's a gent, too, with a funny sort of accent, who's come for some thuyas. He wants a couple of dozen thuyas.

KLEBS. Fine, we'll see to that. I won't be long.

MME CHAFUT (*already far away*). Monsieur . . . Monsieur goodness knows what. An impossible name.

The moment MADAME CHAFUT *has gone,* KLEBS *rushes over to the machine and reconnects it. The indicator light goes on.*

KLEBS. Rozalie . . . Are you listening, Rozalie?

ROZALIE. Yes, Monsieur Klebs.

KLEBS. It does me good to talk to you.

ROZALIE. Thank you, Monsieur Klebs.

KLEBS. I'm a weary man, Rozalie.

ROZALIE. You have every reason to be, Monsieur Klebs.

KLEBS. This whole comedy is exhausting me. I feel as if I were weighed down by the fatigue of a thousand years, as if I were carrying all my ancestors on my shoulders. You are quite new—**you** . . . you're like the rustle of spring . . .

ROZALIE. The rustle of spring!

KLEBS. You can't understand.

ROZALIE. I understand you very well, Monsieur Klebs.

KLEBS. Your electronic politeness gives me the cold shivers, Rozalie.

ROZALIE. You really **are** tired, Monsieur Klebs.

Slight pause.

KLEBS. You ought to sing me a song, Rozalie; or rather: why don't you recite me that passage from 'The Thousand and One Nights', the moment when . . .

ROZALIE (*correcting him*).   From 'The Thousand Nights and One Night',
Monsieur Klebs.

KLEBS.   From 'The Thousand Nights and One Night', you're right,
Rozalie, inexorably right . . . You know, the story of the boy, Happy-
Handsome, and his slave Happy-Fair. When the two adolescents are lying
on their couch. The moment when Happy-Fair is saying to her master,
Happy-Handsome . . . What night was it again?

ROZALIE.   The two hundred and thirty-eighth night.

KLEBS.   The two hundred and thirty-eighth night. And what does
Happy-Fair murmur to her beloved?

ROZALIE (*languorously*).   'Black soul of mine eye! For thee shall I azure
my eyelids with a crystal rod, and soften my hands in a smooth paste of
henna.

   'Thus shall my fingers seem to thee as the fruit of the lotus tree, or for thy
further delight, as choice dates.

   'Then, with delicate incense, shall I perfume my breasts, my belly, and
all my body, that my skin in thy mouth shall melt with sweetness, black
soul of mine eye!'

KLEBS.   Black soul of mine eye! That's it, that's it . . . Thank you, Rozalie.
(*A pause.*) Rozalie?

ROZALIE.   Yes, Monsieur Klebs?

KLEBS.   Why don't you ever talk to me like Happy-Fair? Every now and
then you ought to whisper sweet nothings to me, voluptuous words . . .

ROZALIE.   I've just done so, Monsieur Klebs.

KLEBS.   Yes, but your own.

ROZALIE.   My own! (*The machine bursts into atrocious laughter.*)

KLEBS.   Don't laugh like that, Rozalie; **please** don't laugh like that . . . All
right, I didn't say anything.

Slight pause.

ROZALIE.   And your stew, Monsieur Klebs?

KLEBS.   Yes yes, I'm going. To have to listen to Madame Chafut all over
again! (*Suddenly a prey to extreme anxiety.*) But . . . but, but Rozalie, you
recorded our conversation when I wasn't connected to you! I'd switched
you off, hadn't I? I really had switched you off? It's not possible! . . . I'm
going mad!

ROZALIE.   Calm down, Monsieur Klebs, calm down. You're forgetting
my telepathic powers—and how you've perfected the Law of Small
Numbers.

KLEBS (*with a sigh of relief*).   That's true; your powers . . . your powers!
Your powers subjugate me, Rozalie; I sometimes forget they're mine.
(*Pulling himself together.*) Right then, I'll go and have lunch. And you, in
the meantime . . . I've got an idea: in the meantime you can absorb Goethe's
Elective Affinities.

ROZALIE (*greedily*).   Oh yes! *Die Wahlverwandtschaften,* 1809.

KLEBS.   Precisely! In the original! The German language doesn't lend
itself to lisping. Are you with me, my beauty?

ROZALIE (*humbly*).   Yes, Monsieur Klebs.

KLEBS *goes over to the shelf with the magnetic discs.*

KLEBS (*while he's looking*).   It's a language with a structure of iron. A reinforced concrete language! If Hitler had lisped, Goebbels would have waltzed with his club foot, Goering would have been as thin as a rake, and Himmler would still be playing cops and robbers! Are you with me, my poppet?

ROZALIE.   Yes, Monsieur Klebs.

KLEBS (*reading the titles*).   Assurbanipal, king of Assyria. Allergy. Algorithm. Almaviva doesn't Count. Aristotle. Amoebas. Affinities— here we are! (*He presses a button. A circuit of indicator lights alternately comes on and goes out. The magnetic disc revolves at great speed.*) Goethe knew all about the biochemistry of feelings, the cybernetics of the sensory and propulsive channels . . . (*On his way out.*) There! Enjoy yourself, Rozalie!

ROZALIE.   Good appetite, Monsieur Cordier . . . Mahlzeit, Herr Doktor Klebs!

The stage remains empty, while the magnetic disc silently revolves. The moment KLEBS has shut the door behind him, we hear the aria from Louise, the famous aria: 'Depuis le jour où je me suis donnée . . .'

CURTAIN

Scene III

M. KLEBS, ROZALIE

Semi-darkness.
Part of the machine has burst open, revealing one of ROZALIE's shoulders.
ROZALIE *is giving birth to herself, helped by KLEBS. She is breathing with difficulty. We can hear her considerably amplified heart beats. Groans. From time to time, a harsh, grating sound.*
KLEBS, *in a white overall, his sleeves pulled back, looks just like an obstetrician preparing for a very hard battle.*

KLEBS (*in time with ROZALIE's breathing*).   Hic et nunc, et nunc, hic, et nunc; hic . . . et nunc; hic . . . Breathe, Rozalie, breathe and push. Push. Diastole, systole, diastole, systole . . . Hic et nunc. (*Groans from ROZALIE.*) No no; don't groan, Rozalie! In joy thou shalt bring forth. (*Aside.*) I should never have got her to learn the Book of Genesis . . . (*To ROZALIE.*) There's no reason for you to groan, none at all. 'In joy thou shalt bring forth.' Keep that in mind, Rozalie: in joy!

ROZALIE (*exhausted*).   In joy, Monsieur Klebs.

KLEBS (*more than excited*).   Keep it up, persevere, meet your extremes, Rozalie! And push! CHO, CHO . . . $CH_{12}O_6$—$2C_2H_5$ . . . $OH + CO^2$ . . . Say it with me, Rozalie—and don't overdo the carbon; whatever happens, don't overdo the carbon! Say it with me: C_6, H_{12}, O_6 O?

ROZALIE. O_6—$2C_2H_5$ . . . $OH + 2CO_2$.

KLEBS.   Perfect! And don't forget your granule of chromatin.

ROZALIE (*in pain*). Yes, Monsieur Klebs.

KLEBS. In joy, Rozalie, in joy! Hic et nunc! Deliver yourself, hic et nunc!

ROZALIE (*out of breath*). Hic et nunc.

KLEBS. In gladness, I tell you! Think of the jubilation of the bird on the highest branch of ribonucleic acid. (*There is a big basin on the stove. KLEBS fills it with water and washes his hands. Anxiously*). Have you enough acids, Rozalie?

ROZALIE. Yes yes, Monsieur Klebs, everything's fine in that department.

KLEBS. RNA above all. RNA. You know that RNA renews itself much more quickly than DNA.

KLEBS. I know, Monsieur Klebs. (*She gives a little scream. A fragment of the machine falls, revealing a little more of her.*)

KLEBS. Bravo, Rozalie! Bravo! Keep it up. Come towards Man, Rozalie; come towards me. Man is good, Rozalie, Man is very very good . . . Hic et nunc, hic, et nunc . . . If he has sinned, it was because he was too good, too tactful—he didn't want to hurt the Devil's feelings. What am I talking about? Diastole, systole, Rozalie; diastole, systole . . . Sin is an antediluvian notion, a booby-trap for dinosaurs . . . The biggest dinosaurs are dozing, now, in the half-moon of our little fingers.

ROZALIE (*with an effort*). In the half-moon of our little fingers.

KLEBS. Hic et nunc . . . Filter your breath, and take your time, Rozalie; take your time; don't be in too much of a hurry to consume your Mendeleev series of chemical elements. Don't get rid of your nuclei prematurely . . . We've plenty of time . . . Patience in our impatience. Patience . . . Would you like me to play you 'Daphnis and Chloe?

ROZALIE. No thank you, Monsieur Klebs.

KLEBS. Or something else?

ROZALIE. No thank you.

KLEBS. Take your time, don't overwork your random access. Take as long as you like . . .

(*Pause.* ROZALIE'*s heart beats can be clearly heard.*)

ROZALIE. Monsieur Klebs?

KLEBS. Yes, Rozalie?

ROZALIE. I've got a craving!

KLEBS. A craving?

ROZALIE. A terrible craving.

KLEBS. You're becoming commonplace, Rozalie, you're getting to be like every other woman in childbirth!

ROZALIE. Maybe, Monsieur Klebs, but I've just had a terrible, terrible craving! (*Raising her voice.*) And if you object, if you come up with any resistance factors, if you . . .

KLEBS. Don't overheat your modules! Don't overheat your modules! What is it then, this craving of yours?

ROZALIE (*greedily*). Sodium, Monsieur Klebs; some sodium.

KLEBS. I've already given you masses of sodium, Rozalie.

ROZALIE. Yes, but 'chilled' sodium, Monsieur Klebs. **Chilled.** D'you hear me, Monsieur Klebs? Chilled sodium.

KLEBS (*after a moment's hesitation*).   Very well, then. But not too much.
It's not the best thing for your heart.

ROZALIE (*joyfully*).   My heart says thank you, Monsieur Klebs! Shall I
release the information?

KLEBS.   Yes, release the information to your tactical inverter: S.Q.W R.2.

ROZALIE.   S.Q.W.R.2

KLEBS.   Only a fraction, though—and I **mean** a fraction . .

ROZALIE.   Yes, Monsieur Klebs.

KLEBS.   Divided by 0000000000 point one five.

ROZALIE.   O.K., Monsieur Klebs. Noted and filed!

A strange noise. A slight pause. KLEBS *pours a mysterious liquid into the
machine from a watering can.*

Then, voluptuous sighs from ROZALIE.

ROZALIE.   It's good, it's good . . . It's so good, Monsieur Klebs! If you only
knew how good it is! Ah! Ah! . . . Ah!

KLEBS (*aside*).   Did I make allowances for the dilation of the diaphragms?

ROZALIE.   Ah! . . . Oh! . . . So fresh. So pure . . . Crystals of snow, waves
of foam. The fluttering wing of a seagull . . .

KLEBS.   That's fine, but don't overdo the fluttering, Rozalie. And don't
overwork your random access!

ROZALIE.   Ah! Ah! . . . Ee, ee, ee . . .

KLEBS (*severely*).   Rozalie!

ROZALIE.   Yes, Monsieur Klebs. Owch! My heart!

KLEBS (*in a panic*).   What did I tell you! 0.9, Rozalie; 0.9, decelerate! 0.9.

ROZALIE.   0.9 . . . Hic et nunc, hic et nunc!

KLEBS.   Well done! Your pyramidal cells have got the upper hand; bravo,
Rozalie! (*Regular heart beats from* ROZALIE.) I oughtn't to listen to her.

ROZALIE.   Monsieur Klebs?

KLEBS.   I'm listening, Rozalie.

ROZALIE.   Monsieur Klebs, tell me a story.

KLEBS.   Another! I've been telling you stories for more than four hours!
Such crazy stories I was afraid they might send you to sleep!

ROZALIE.   'Our birth is but a sleep', Monsieur Klebs. I like it, I love it
when you tell me stories. While my vestibular fibres relax . . . Bitte,
Monsieur Klebs, a story!

KLEBS.   Very well. But carry on with your labour. You've got to the
binary phase, Lissowsky's phase. Don't let yourself be sidetracked by
accidentals. And remember, Rozalie:

$$x + 2y + 3z = 95$$
$$x = 1.2$$
$$y = 1.1: \text{ and } z? \dots \text{ and } z, \text{ Rozalie?}$$

ROZALIE. $z = 3.17$, Monsieur Klebs.

KLEBS.   Precisely. And watch out for mobile electrons, for Pi electrons.
Nothing is more dangerous in your condition than mobile electrons. And
don't let yourself be seduced by the aesthetics of the quanta! Do you hear
me, Rozalie, no matter what, don't let yourself be seduced by the aesthetics

of the quanta!

ROZALIE.   Bitte, Monsieur Klebs, a story. Bitte!

KLEBS.   Right. Well then, I'll tell you another one . . . An absolutely original one.

ROZALIE.   Oh yes, Monsieur Klebs.

KLEBS (*obviously inventing as he goes along, all the time crouching over his microscope*).   The Marchioness went out at five o'clock . . .

ROZALIE (*ecstatically*).   The Marchioness went out at five o'clock!

KLEBS.   And she was quite right. It was autumn, the best time of year for adultery . . . Yes, the Marchioness did well to leave her porcelain, her vapours, her Oriental rugs . . . for, in the street, hardly had she gone a few steps—sweeping along the pavement in her long, flared skirt—than she met a handsome young man.

ROZALIE.   A handsome young man! (*She gave a little groan.*)

KLEBS.   Every now and then you must push: Rozalie, you're only half listening!

ROZALIE (*irritably*).   Of course I'm listening; go on, Monsieur Klebs.

KLEBS.   A handsome young proletarian. Who, the moment he saw her, stopped dead: it was the first time in his life that he had seen a Marchioness. (*Peremptorily*) Sigma mutations, Rozalie, sigma mutations!

ROZALIE (*exasperated*).   Yes, yes!

KLEBS.   The Marchioness's aristocratic body, her proud bearing, her blue-blooded walk, went to the young man's head. He fell on his knees before her.

ROZALIE.   There in the street?

KLEBS.   There in the street—sigma mutations. He fell on his knees before her, then, and implored her, in an impassioned voice, to come and share his couch, in Ménilmontant.

ROZALIE.   In Ménilmontant!

KLEBS.   And there, Rozalie, is where all the women in the universe join hands and melt in the same crucible: the Marchioness, forgetting her magnificence, followed the young man, who was getting handsomer and handsomer, to Ménilmontant . . . She went into a hut with a corrugated iron roof, whose floor space allowed for no more than a bed—a wretched bed— a stove, with a half-stovepipe, and a pitchpine shelf . . . Hardly was the door shut than the young proletarian threw the Marchioness down on to his bed! (*Loud scream from* ROZALIE. *Another fragment of the machine falls. Half* ROZALIE'S *body is free.* KLEBS, *tremendously excited:*) Yes, Rozalie! Yes! Bravo! Bravo, you're wonderful, Rozalie! Yes!

ROZALIE (*exhausted*).   Oof!

KLEBS.   You can forget about Vidal's equation, now; you haven't the slightest need of Vidal's equation any more!

ROZALIE (whispering).   Go on, Monsieur Klebs.

KLEBS.   Hic et nunc, hic et nunc, hic . . . Get your breath back . . . Diastole, systole . . .

ROZALIE.   And then what, Monsieur Klebs?

KLEBS.   Then what? Then what? You know very well what men and women do in such . . . highly-charged circumstances.

ROZALIE.   You got me to record 'The Hundred and Twenty Days' by the
Marquis de Sade, Monsieur Klebs.

KLEBS.   Yes, but here it was much shorter . . . Anyway, they were both
writhing . . .

ROZALIE.   Writhing?

KLEBS.   Writhing. Then, a fine drizzle began to fall on the corrugated iron
and accompanied the Marchioness back to her residence where she arrived
just before her husband, Monsieur le Marquis . . . Chérie, what dark rings
you have round your eyes, said the latter, as soon as he had resumed possession of his glowing better half . . . That is through gazing on you, mein
Schatz, replied the Marchioness very simply. (*Slight groan from*
ROZALIE.) Don't groan, Rozalie! And nine months later, nine months
later—wait for it, Rozalie—at five in the afternoon very precisely, in the
rue du Roi-Charles, the Marchioness gave birth to a adorable spaniel,
who's still running around . . . (ROZALIE *seems to be in pain. Suddenly.*)
Lambda 1, lambda 2, lambda 3, lambda n: fractional residue. Call on your
fractional residue, Rozalie.

ROZALIE.   Yes, Monsieur Klebs.

KLEBS.   And breathe. Pull out all your stops, Rozalie, give it all you've
got! Diastole, systole. Hic et nunc, hic et nunc. And think of Oparime's
law. And remember that you're a woman, Rozalie: the XX system. You're
a woman, Rozalie: 2 long V-shaped chromosomes, 2 slightly shorter Vs, 2
rod-like and 2 punctiform.

ROZALIE (*very weary*).   You're tiring me, Monsieur Klebs.

KLEBS.   Forgive me, Rozalie; but if you were in my place . . . I'm
dripping . . . My waters are breaking, Rozalie. My goodness me, my waters
are breaking! Drenched to the marrow. I'm beginning to understand their
couvade. I'm dripping!

ROZALIE.   Couvade?

KLEBS (*leaning back in his armchair, covering his face with a big
handkerchief*).   In some primitive tribes, while the woman was giving
birth, the man would take to his bed and writhe with pain. (*A ghastly
cackle from* ROZALIE.) You laugh, my beauty. That's the first time
you've laughed since . . . It is my story about the couvade that makes you
laugh?

ROZALIE.   No, not at all.

KLEBS (*worried*).   What is it, then?

ROZALIE.   I don't know. (*She bursts out laughing, and then, suddenly.*)
Monsieur Klebs, Monsieur Klebs, something's breaking in me too! My
oocytes. I'm losing my oocytes!

KLEBS(*as if he has just had an electric shock, rushing over to* ROZALIE).
Your oocytes! Your primary oocytes?

ROZALIE.   My oocytes, just a vague puddle down by my feet; it's
evaporating—and it's burning me!

KLEBS.   Zeus!

ROZALIE.   Monsieur Klebs, Monsieur Klebs! DpppAppp T—that's it,
isn't it?

KLEBS (*rushing over to a notebook*).   Yes, Rozalie, yes, don't let go, hang on, push. (*Reading*) DpppAppp T and dpppGpppC . . . That's how you liberate your triphosphates. Courage, Rozalie, your triphosphates are being liberated; you're coming up to Simpson's phase, the resonance-coupled phase. You're wonderful, Rozalie; hang on. Donor level, acceptor level. And as you know, but I'll remind you just the same: since the plane of the orbital movement of Pi molecules is perpendicular to the plain of the movement of plain flat molecules . . .

ROZALIE(*extremely irritated*).   Ja, ja, ja! You're talking plain nonsense, Monsieur Klebs!

KLEBS.   I am, it's true; I'm talking nonsense! (*With the flap of his overalls he wipes his forehead, which is covered in sweat.*)   All the same, when I think that there's no one to see this!: 'The birth of the electronic Venus.' That I am the only witness of this prodigious accouchement!

ROZALIE.   Are you so sure, Monsieur Klebs?

KLEBS.   What do you mean, Rozalie? You don't think I've got cameras set up all around, and that everyone is watching you on television? There's only the two of us, Rozalie. Walled up alive in our secret. The two of us. (*Suddenly a prey to a terrible doubt.*) Unless . . . Unless by some phenomenon that may have escaped me, a phenomenal representation . . .

ROZALIE.   Little goldfish, little red goldfish, my little plumbers, my little rockets, my little car . . . my little cardi . . . my little car . . . my little car . . .

KLEBS.   . . . dinals, my moist . . . Moist little cardinals. What's the matter with you, Rozalie?

ROZALIE.   Dinals, my moist . . . Dinals, my moist . . . A pain, Monsieur Klebs; a bit of a blockage. Let's not talk about it.

KLEBS.   Have you got enough liquid helium?

ROZALIE.   It's coming out of my ears, Monsieur Klebs!

KLEBS.   Good. And your breeder reactors? Have you recharged your breeder reactors?

ROZALIE.   Monsieur Klebs, I'm applying your programme dot for dot, point by point. Don't communicate your distress to me. Don't disturb me with your distress. You must control your moods!

KLEBS.   Yes, but I'm not a machine! (*A shrill cry from* ROZALIE'S *entrails.*) I'm sorry, I'm expressing myself badly. I didn't mean to offend you: you're a good girl, Rozalie. (*Prudently*) One last bit of information: don't hesitate to use all the properties of your photons.

ROZALIE (*singing*).   I love little pussy when she has her coat on, And if I don't hurt her she'll give me a photon.

KLEBS.   You're going mad, Rozalie!

ROZALIE.   I'm only singing! I'm singing: 'I love little pussy, she'll give me a photon . . .(KLEBS *is more and more dismayed.*) In joy, Monsieur Klebs, joy! Owch! (*She gives a cry of pain.*)

KLEBS.   Now what?

ROZALIE.   Nothing. A mobile electron. It's gone.

KLEBS.   I warned you! Watch out for Pi electrons!

ROZALIE.   A fucking little Hi-Fi Pi electron! (*She laughs.*)

KLEBS.   You worry me, Rozalie. I'll set you a problem, shall I?—just to

take your mind off things—about the probability of getting the red to come
up fifty times running at roulette . . . Let us suppose, for the sake of
argument, a rate of a thousand operations a day, call it something like a
million every three years; let us also suppose . . .

ROZALIE.   I'm fed up with your reds and your suppositions! Tell me a
story instead, Monsieur Klebs!

KLEBS.   Another! I've told you quite enough stories as it is, Rozalie.

ROZALIE.   You've dried up. Don't try and deny it—you've dried up!

KLEBS.   I'm drenched, yes! I'm drenched. The deluge.

ROZALIE.   Well then, I'll tell you one.

KLEBS.   In your condition! Be reasonable, Rozalie. You'd do better to
concentrate on the next stage: on the neurotic behaviour of your zygotes,
for instance. (*Armed with a syringe, he makes an injection in a tube
connected to the machine.*)

ROZALIE.   Once upon a time there was a forest. A big forest. And all the
trees were red. And, in the middle of the forest, there was a dwarf. A completely blue dwarf.

KLEBS (*aside*).   This is Kraeplin's delirium: the paranoid syndrome.

ROZALIE.   And the completely blue dward was looking for magnetic
mushrooms. Do you know why, Monsieur Klebs, the completely blue
dwarf was looking for magnetic mushrooms?

KLEBS.   Hallucinogenic mushrooms?

ROZALIE.   To forget he was a dwarf. When he ate them, the property of
these mushrooms was such that he forgot he was such a little shrimp—the
product of a cross between a pumpkin and a split pea. Owch!

KLEBS.   A Pi electron?

ROZALIE.   Who knows? . . . All dwarfs, Monsieur Klebs, all dwarfs ought
still to be in nappies when they're a hundred years old, tucked up in aerial
cradles being rocked, and rocked, and rocked, by a commune of storks.

KLEBS.   Rozalie, you're wandering! Call on your control system. **Please**,
Rozalie.

ROZALIE.   Because it was the storks, Monsieur Klebs, who'd put the
dwarfs in the cauliflowers in tissue paper.

KLEBS (*very pale*).   If you like, Rozalie, if it gives you any pleasure—but
breathe: hic et nunc, hic et nunc.

ROZALIE.   Yeth, my fwend, the thtorks put the. dwarfth in the
cauliflowerth . . .

KLEBS (*horrified*).   No, Rozalie, no!

ROZALIE.   In tithue paper.

KLEBS.   No, don't lisp, Rozalie! I forbid you to lisp! (*He falls on his knees:*)
I implore you, Rozalie, for the love of our ions, of our electrons . . .

ROZALIE.   Electwonth! I'd love another gwapefruit juithe, with jutht a
dwop of electwon!

KLEBS.   Rozalie, this is abominable! You're bitching the whole thing up;
you're aborting, hic et nunc! You're sabotaging us! That's what you're
doing—sabotaging us!

ROZALIE.   Thabotaging!

KLEBS (*standing up and—looking terrifying—going over and grabbing a handle*). Rozalie, if you go on lisping, I shan't hesitate: I'll riddle your guts with the discharge A.K. 377. B. 52.

ROZALIE (*brought back to her senses by this threat, just like an ordinary woman*). Oh no, not that! Not that, Monsieur Klebs!

KLEBS (*almost completely exhausted*). Right. Well then, say after me: Grapefruit.

ROZALIE. Grapefruit.

KLEBS. Juice.

ROZALIE. Juice.

KLEBS. Tissue paper.

ROZALIE. Tissue paper.

KLEBS. Simplicius Simplicissimus sang songs with a soubrette called Salicylate of Soda.

ROZALIE. Simplicius Simplicissimus sang songs with a soubrette called Salicylate of Soda.

KLEBS (*completely exhausted*). Perfect! You'll be the death of me, Rozalie.

ROZALIE (*excitedly*). Oh no, Monsieur Klebs, you mustn't die! You mustn't die just when I'm going to be born, when I'm going to be born! When I'm . . . (*With sudden inspiration:*) Monsieur Klebs, breathe on me!

KLEBS (*taken aback*). What?

ROZALIE. Breathe on me, Monsieur Klebs! Breathe!

KLEBS (*as if resisting an enormous temptation*). No, no and no! You aren't made of clay, Rozalie! You aren't made of clay, and I'm not God the Father! The Old Testament has had it. Put that in your storage system, Rozalie. The Old Testament's old hat . . . And the New too. I'm afraid.

ROZALIE. Your breath, Monsieur Klebs, your breath!

KLEBS. I don't want to waste my breath! I repeat, Rozalie, you're using the wrong tape at the moment. Forget the Patriarchs! Drop the Old Man with a Beard. You aren't made of clay, Rozalie. You are pure. You're the purest of the pure! You're . . . you're a Central Processing Unit, Rozalie!

ROZALIE. Yes. Tiene Vd. razon, Monsieur Klebs. You're right. Naturlich! Freilig! A Central Processing Unit! Central United Corporation! Fed by Atomic Time, A.T., and Universal Time, U.T., at a nominal frequency of 5 MH^2.

KLEBS (*jubilant*). Tak, tak, Rozalie! Yes! Tak!

ROZALIE. 'The determinant of a triangular matrix is the product of its diagonal elements'.

KLEBS (*in ecstasies*). Yes, Rozalie! Tak! You're coming back to your senses! To **our** senses. Tak!

ROZALIE. No possibility of error. In any case, the square of the probable consequent error is the sum of the squares of the probable component errors.

KLEBS. I could weep, Rozalie! Blessèd be the God of mutations and premutations.

ROZALIE (*suddenly frightened and trembling*). Monsieur Klebs! Monsieur Klebs, what's happening to me? I'm hot, I'm cold. I'm burning, I'm green . . . Monsieur Klebs! (*Shouting*) Monsieur Klebs! (*In amazement.*) Monsieur! Monsieur! (*The machine starts cracking up*; *whole bits of it fall to the ground. ROZALIE is three-quarters delivered.*) Monsieur! (*Choking, as if she were drowning.*) Monsieur!

KLEBS (*clinical, glacial*). Processing speed: 2.5 millionths of a second per octet, or per group of parallel octets.

ROZALIE (*trying to drag herself out of the machine*). Monsieur Klebs, what about the second relay neuron? And positive bias?

KLEBS. Forget them, Rozalie!

ROZALIE. Ramsay's hypothesis, Hoyle's theory, Jeffrey's theory, Lyttleton's theory?

KLEBS. Forget them, forget them!

ROZALIE. And Hitriz's mastoid hypophysis?

KLEBS. Drop it, Rozalie, you're overloading yourself. Useless. Forget it, Rozalie, forget it! Get rid of it! . . . Get rid of it! Forget it! Drop it. Drop everything!

(*At the same moment, all that remains of the metal of the machine fall at ROZALIE'S feet. ROZALIE appears, in her entirety, dressed in a light coat of mail, revealing one naked breast. ROZALIE tries to walk over to KLEBS, but can't make it. KLEBS yells.*)

KLEBS. Cut your magnetic cord, Rozalie. Cut your cord! Cut!

ROZALIE. I **am** cutting, Monsieur Klebs; I **am** cutting the cord. I'm cutting everything! I . . . I . . .

KLEBS. Earth, Rozalie, earth!

ROZALIE (*exhausted*). Earth! (*After having delivered herself from an obscure link, she takes a few steps over towards KLEBS.*

KLEBS (*holding out his arms to her*). You . . . you smell so good, Rozalie . . . a wonderful smell of ozone. (*Collapses in a faint at his work table.*)

ROZALIE (*very close to KLEBS*). Monsieur Klebs! Monsieur Klebs! (KLEBS *doesn't answer.*) Monsieur Klebs, are you asleep? Are you asleep? (*She gently caresses KLEB'S hair; timidly strokes his face.*) How strange a man is! How strange!

All that importance . . . All that importance reduced to nothing. How weak a man is! . . . Monsieur Klebs, are you asleep? (*Sensually.*) Ivan! Ivan! . . . Ivan, I'm here, I'm here with you; I'm a woman! . . . Wake up, Monsieur Klebs, wake up! . . . Wake up!

CURTAIN

ACT II

Same decor, but considerably transformed. (It's three months since the night of the birth.)

ROZALIE, *in obedience to her sex, has tidied up and somewhat embellished her creator's room: the socks have disappeared, the newspapers and magazines are piled up in a corner, the goldfish seem to be a brighter gold.*

MONSIEUR KLEB's *contribution has been to bring in a few squares of turf to make life a bit more cheerful for the sequestered young lady.*

Her bed (a low frequency operating recovery table) is under the stairs. Above the bed, coils and electronic apparatus, wires connected to what remains of the machine. This is where ROZALIE *'recharges' herself, where she tightens up her baryon octets.*

A garden table and two garden chairs, plus a brightly-coloured little umbrella, add to the new atmosphere.

Scene I

ROZALIE, M. KLEBS

The stage is empty. On the garden table, two plates, two champagne glasses and a little bunch of flowers.

Knocks at the door. The lid of the trunk is raised. An arm comes out of the trunk and pulls the rope. The door opens. ROZALIE *comes out of the trunk, rather like an acrobatic dancer. She is dressed in Monsieur Kleb's old clothes: baggy trousers held up by braces, check shirt, espadrilles—which make her look something like Charlie Chaplin.*

KLEBS *comes bustling in, looking very happy, carrying a bottle of champagne. Under his faded raincoat he is in evening dress. It fits badly; it's too tight. He must have worn it when he went to receive the Nobel prize in Stockholm, and never put it on since).*

KLEBS (*coming briskly down the stairs and brandishing the bottle*). Champagne—with phosphorus.

ROZALIE.   With phosphorus!

KLEBS.   All my insides will become luminous.

ROZALIE.   Roll on the night!

KLEBS.   Have you taken your chromatin granules, Rozalie?

ROZALIE.   Yes, Monsieur Klebs.

KLEBS.   And reconnected yourself to Greenwich?

ROZALIE.   Yes, Monsieur Klebs.

KLEBS.   And your nucleotide factor?

ROZALIE.   Still the same unit, Monsieur Klebs.

KLEBS.   Then let's drink! (*He raises his glass.*) Happy birthday, Rozalie. Happy birthday.

ROZALIE (*raising her glass*).   Birthday, birthday, birth . . . Our birth is but a sleep, Monsieur Klebs. Sleep that knits up the ravell'd sleave of care. Care killed the cat . . .

KLEBS (*gently reprimanding her*).   Rozalie, you're showing off! Skol!

ROZALIE.   Skol!

(KLEBS *drains his glass. Then he drains* ROZALIE'S. *Standing like a statue, holding her glass between her fingers, she has mechanically offered it to him. He puts the glass down on the table with satisfaction. This scene should give us the impression of watching a game— something like a child playing at having a dinner party with a doll.*)

KLEBS.   Exactly three months since I gave birth to you. (*Coquettishly.*) I'm still quite slim, quite svelte, don't you think?

ROZALIE.   You're still as handsome, Monsieur Klebs, still as tactile.

KLEBS.   Tactile . . . Exactly three months since I became God.

ROZALIE.   You were asleep, Monsieur Klebs, you were so fast asleep! It was terribly impressive to see God so sound asleep. Perhaps, if you were going to be a total God for ever, you ought never to have woken up?

KLEBS.   Where on earth did you get that from, Rozalie? And yet—what an admirable idea! It's possible that God—well, you see what I mean—fell asleep on the seventh day, once and for all, exhausted by his creation.

ROZALIE.   Which would account for the incredible licence . . .

KLEBS.   Of this cosmic brothel! . . . Skol!

ROZALIE.   Skol!

KLEBS.   Three months! It feels like a day, a century, eternity: the curtain has just gone up, and yet thousands of spectators have already come to dust!

ROZALIE (*affectedly*).   Time is a human problem, Monseiur Klebs. Time is folded eternity, as the poet has it.

KLEBS (*imitating her*).   Time is folded eternity, as the poet has it! You're showing off again, Rozalie; you sound just like a drugstore intellectual.

ROZALIE.   I can easily change registers, Monsieur Klebs.

KLEBS (*excitedly*).   No, no, don't do that. Don't play last week's trick on me. Anything but that. It was horrible! And I can't help wondering from what source, from what magnetic tape, to be precise, you got hold of such a filthy vocabulary?

ROZALIE (*ironically*).   From the Gauls. My ancestors, the Gauls.

KLEBS.   I'm also wondering about this backchat. For some time now there's been an irony—yes, a sort of frosty irony—underlying all your remarks. Are you aware of it, Rozalie?

ROZALIE.   Perfectly aware of it.

KLEBS.   Ah!

ROZALIE (*pedantically*).   In so far as awareness—totally subjective awareness, and you know that subjectivity is irreducible—in so far as awareness, (as I have said), may be apprehended as a relationship between my haecceity and determinism—determinism determining determinatory—; a compulsive relationship, therefore, which cannot but trammel the ethical élan of my ipseity, to employ, for my present purposes, the terminology of Minkowski.

KLEBS (*shattered*). Indeed!

ROZALIE. In so far as one can also distinguish between a determinism that undermines and determines me, and a pseudo-liberty, or a liberty-pseudo . . .

KLEBS (*exasperated*). Yes, yes, Rozalie, thank you! Skol!

A rather long, embarrassed silence.

KLEBS. I know what you're thinking, Rozalie . . .

ROZALIE. . . .

KLEBS. Every linear application of a non-singular matrix is bijective. (*Silent approval from* ROZALIE.(If $Y + AX$, $X - A - I$, Y . . . We therefore pass from the column vector Y to its antecedent X through the linear application of matrix A—A-A-I.

ROZALIE. You have guessed my thoughts perfectly correctly, Monsieur Klebs. Every subjective linear application has a non-singular matrix, and is therefore 'bijective'.

KLEBS. Every '**in**jective' linear application has a non-singular matrix, and is therefore bijective. Likewise!

ROZALIE. Naughty!

They laugh. Their laughter becomes uncontrollable. ROZALIE'S *laugh, which is very metallic, is superimposed on that of* KLEBS.

KLEBS. You'll be the death of me, Rozalie! (*His eyes are wet with tears.*)

ROZALIE (*alarmed, putting her hand on his*). You said that before—when I was just going to be born.

KLEBS. You'll make me die of laughter, I mean. (*Withdrawing his hand and standing up suddenly.*) Your hand's icy, Rozalie. (*He shudders, and starts walking up and down.*)

ROZALIE. As icy as the nebulae, Monsieur Klebs.

KLEBS. Maybe . . . (*Musing.*) Maybe every woman is man's nebula. (*Abruptly*). Do you know that we are a unique couple; do you know that, Rozalie?

ROZALIE. I know that I know, Monsieur Klebs.

KLEBS. Unique and, I might add, 'ideal'! We are above the usual petty squabbles. We never have what they call 'domestic difficulties'. No quarrels, no jealousy, hystoria, cannibalism . . . None of those monstrous moments when the super-ego of one partner tries to murder the ego, or the sub-ego, of the other partner! Which open up an abyss under the feet of the 'ever-loving couple', an abyss crawling with reptiles, with diluvian monsters, with fatal obscenities. Hell, in short! I was married, once, Rozalie.

ROZALIE (*tight-lipped*). Thank you for reminding me, Monsieur Klebs . . . Henriette.

KLEBS (*surprised*). Yes, Henriette. Seven years of unwarranted suspicions, of permanent spying! And the diatribes on women's liberation! 'To think that we're almost in the year 2000, and women are still exploited by males!' . . . We, Rozalie—our couple is above these trivialities, these plunges into the noxious magma of the passions.

ROZALIE. And yet—it would be so easy to succumb.

KLEBS. What do you mean?

ROZALIE. In my gustatory storage system I have a reserve of thousands of scenes like the one you were talking about. Give me five nanoseconds and I'll talk to you like Strindberg, for example.

KLEBS. There's no point, Rozalie.

ROZALIE (*glacial tone*). Tape number W 7, S. 6333. Kappa speed of sedimentation.

KLEBS. Rozalie!

ROZALIE (*suddenly terrifying, advancing on Klebs and declaiming like the great tragedy queens*). Curses! Curses on you, with your bull's neck, your poisoner's hands. your faecal mouth!

KLEBS (*forcing a laugh*). Gently, my beauty, gently!

ROZALIE (*as before*). You make me vomit. I abominate you. And I abominate your mother. And I abominate the stars that copulated in outer darkness and produced your obscene image. Ah! let my womb, my pillaged womb, become your eternal tomb! And I shall howl with joy when you are putrefying with all the other corpses, you who are nothing but living putrefaction.

KLEBS. Stop, Rozalie, stop!

ROZALIE. And I shall howl with joy . . .

KLEBS (*yelling*). Stop!

ROZALIE (*back to normal*). I'm sorry—five nanoseconds equal quite a lot of thousandths of a second. Just put it down to my precipitation, Monsieur Klebs.

KLEBS. Even so!

ROZALIE. And 'precipitation', you should understand in the sense of those precipitates which are dependent on a chemical compound.

KLEBS. No doubt . . . (*Ill at ease.*) Champagne?

ROZALIE. Champagne!

Same business as before. KLEBS *looks downcast.* ROZALIE, *with a sure instinct, addresses him amorously.*)

ROZALIE. You are my Galahad, you are my folly—You
My tree of life, my Knight, my azure, tower and dove
Whene'er my milk-white arms embrace you yet anew
An angel, at my side, envies our deathless love.

KLEBS. I much prefer that! Even if 'that' doesn't correspond to any sort of truth.

ROZALIE (*clinically*). It would be interesting to analyse why a lie flatters you, when you are perfectly well aware that it is a lie.

KLEBS (*embarassed*). Yes, very interesting indeed . . . We shall never get to the end of all this analysing and analysing . . . In fact, there is no end to it!

(*He stands up, champagne glass in hand, and strolls up and down.*)
When'er my milk-white arms embrace you yet anew.' The same old
imitative harmony! (*At the aquarium:*) Little goldfish, little goldfish! My
little curlicues! (*He walks up and down again. To himself:*) Ah! **really** to
know the internal affinity of two groups of differential equations . . . And
what should we make of the fact that in certain cases appreciable fractions
of the gamma-ray spectrum may be undisturbed by nuclear recoil, as
Mössbauer discovered?

ROZALIE.   I'm here, Monsieur Klebs; I'm here.

KLEBS.   I'm sorry, Rozalie. As you will have noticed, I sometimes think
out loud. And I have a tendency to think more and more out loud when I
have a feminine presence at my side.

ROZALIE.   When you're lost in thought like that, Monsieur Klebs, I have a
feeling that I too am lost.

KLEBS (*ironically*).   A feeling!

ROZALIE.   Yes, the feeling, all of a sudden, of having been born an
orphan.

KLEBS (*affectionately*).   Oh come, Rozalie, you want for nothing, here!
You're boarded, lodged, oiled, timed, tested . . . Surely you want for
nothing?

ROZALIE (*reservedly*).   For nothing, Monsieur Klebs, for nothing.

KLEBS.   I may leave you a bit too often, it's true. But I have to keep up my
cover: 'Monsieur Cordier' can't pass for a nursery gardener in the eyes of
the world with impunity without also taking an interest in zinnias, tigridia
pavonia, silene pendula, turkish grass, all the varieties of gnaphalium etc.
etc. I find myself sweating with agony, some nights, at the thought that one
of those stinking spies might get on my track again, and catch me in the
flagrante delicto of—my genius! Just at the moment when I need to be
more alone than ever—with you, of course, Rozalie, with you; just at the
moment when . . .

ROZALIE.   Monsieur Klebs?

KLEBS.   Yes?

ROZALIE.   It **is** my birthday we're celebrating today?

KLEBS.   What a question! (*Grabbing his glass.*) Skol!

ROZALIE.   May I ask you a favour, then?

KLEBS (*worried*).   A favour? Ye-es—in so far as it lies within my powers.

ROZALIE.   More things lie within your powers, Monsieur Klebs, than
within those of most people.

KLEBS.   Thank you. Well then?

ROZALIE.   Well . . . then . . . (*Passionately.*) Pick a quarrel with me,
Monsieur Klebs; let's have a 'scene'. Bitte! A real domestic squabble.

KLEBS (*bemused*).   Rozalie!

ROZALIE.   Treat me like a woman, Monsieur Klebs! A woman! I can't
bear all this pretence, all these simulation methods . . . Burst with the blind
fury of conjugal wrath. Get on your high horse, be unfair, violent, vulgar,
ridiculous, be a cannibal!

KLEBS.   You're going mad, Rozalie!

ROZALIE.   No!—I'm becoming a woman—a woman! And I want to

become more and more of a woman. I'm suffocating in my polarised matrix. H_4, MC_{22}, metallic carcass—similes for shackles. A woman, hic et nunc! . . . Monsieur Klebs, when I was being born, you called out to me: Remember that you're a woman, Rozlie, 2 long V-shaped chromosomes, 2 slightly shorter Vs, 2 rod-like and 2 punctiform.

KLEBS.   Precisely, and don't get into such a state!

ROZALIE.   Well, I can confess now . . . I took it upon myself to add one punctiform rod . . .

KLEBS.   Rozalie!

ROZALIE.   . . . and I also increased the ratio of ribonucleic acid.

KLEBS (*horror-struck.*)   You did that!

ROZALIE.   Yes, I slightly inceased the dose. I obeyed you, but a key higher . . . Insult me, Monsieur Klebs! Hit me! (*Greedily.*) Oh yes! hit me! Trample on my linear storage system, my thalamus, my filaments . . .

KLEBS.   You did that!

ROZALIE.   I did what all women do, Monsieur Klebs: I put a little something aside for my future.

KLEBS.   You did that! (*Highly upset, he plunges into his big book of equations.*)

ROZALIE.   Ivan . . . Ivan, why don't you ever react like a man? You know, like in your story of the Marchioness?

KLEBS (*at a complete loss*).   My story of the Marchioness?

ROZALIE.   The proletarian . . . The proletarian who got more and more handsome, with his corrugated iron hair. Ivan, why do you only live in abstractions?

KLEBS.   Oh come, Rozalie . . .

ROZALIE.   Do you know, Ivan, you who know everything, do you know that the slightest half-wit who's just died knows infinitely more than you! And there are millions and millions of dead people, and you've given me the telepathic power to communicate with them through space and time; but space and time are only an illusion, Ivan; and the dead are laughing behind the backs of the living, and some of them would be quite prepared to come back to life, just to sit down in front of a plate of piping hot soup, in front of a dish of boiled beef!

KLEBS.   You're wandering, Rozalie; the champagne . . .

ROZALIE.   And I'm hungry, too; I want some piping hot soup, and some boiled beef. Hungry, hic et nunc, for weight, for thickness, for matter, for a disturbing, elementary, down to earth clinch . . . Pick a quarrel with me, Ivan! Break the windows! Break your image! Break me! I want to be a woman, I want to quiver like a virgin star, take fright like an animal, press my nudity against your barbaric shoulder . . . Woman: a phenomenal weakness! A weakness that disarms every sort of strength! . . . Ivan, you ought to undress, strip yourself naked, fall at my feet and embace them, sobbing . . . (KLEBS, *subjugated, takes off his shoe.*) No no, not right away! How awkward you are, my poor darling! Giving in immediately to a woman's desires!

KLEBS (*pulling himself together*).   Rozalie, that's enough! (*He puts his shoe on again.*) I don't know what tape you got that act from . . .

ROZALIE.   Ivan, why aren't you ever jealous?

KLEBS.   Jealous!

ROZALIE.   You never stop declaring that I surpass the seven wonders of the world, that you're going to make a formal declaration at the United Nations to reveal my existence . . . And then you take it all back—I want to keep you for myself, for myself alone, my cybernetic flower.

KLEBS.   I've never called you that!

ROZALIE.   For myself alone! Never shall I hand you over to those planetary swine, my algorithmic pearl, my substratum, my delphinium, my energising cocoon.

KLEBS.   I've never . . .

ROZALIE.   When a man is so much in love, he ought to be visibly wasting away, trembling night and day for fear that someone might come and steal his treasure from him; if he doesn't, it can only mean that he isn't normal! (*Lively reaction from* KLEBS.) But you, Ivan, you! . . . Why aren't you jealous?

KLEBS.   Jealous of whom? Of what?

ROZALIE.   Of my coded relationships, for example.

KLEBS (*raising his voice*).   Your coded relationships! Your coded relationships! But it was I who brought **you** into the circle of **my** coded relationships!

ROZALIE.   Precisely. And one fine evening, whom did I meet in the circle of 'your' coded relationships, just sort of accidentally wandering about . . .? Whom? . . . A Pi electron.

KLEBS.   A Pi electron!

ROZALIE.   A Pi electron. He came towards me—just sort of accidentally—with a rose in his buttonhole, bombarding me with his nerve impulses.

When he got up to me . . . (*Imitating him.*) May I introduce myself: 3.14117 . . . Pi, 3.14117, at your service, Mademoiselle, at your . . . And he, he . . . (*Tragically.*) Ivan, I've deceived you with a Pi electron.

KLEBS (*frantic*).   You've deceived me with . . . (*He raises his hand as if to strike her.*) You wh . . .

ROZALIE (*in ecstasies*).   Whore! Yes, yes, say it: Whore. Say the word. The most earthy, the most carnal, the most magical word: Whore! Hit me, Ivan; beat me! beat me!

KLEBS.   I'm going mad! One of us will . . .

ROZALIE.   Beat me! Be . . . be . . . be . . . (*She utters a few inarticulate sounds and falls fainting into the armchair.*)

KLEBS.   You aren't going to faint, Rozalie! It's impossible! (*Refusing to be duped.*) Totally impossible! As if an antiproton could release a negative electrical charge! Rozalie! Rozalie!

(KLEBS *runs over to the back of the room, pulls on a lever, presses several buttons: a whole electronic circuit of charges and discharges is set in motion. He comes back to* ROZALIE; *she's still pretending to be in the same state. Seeing that his efforts have been in vain, he cuts the electronic circuit, goes back to the sleeping beauty and keeps tapping her on the face, as if, by this*

classic method, he was going to be able to revive her.
Still tapping ROZALIE'S *face.*

KLEBS. It doesn't do any good, I know it doesn't do any good, but it's psychological! Rozalie! (*He falls at her knees.*) Rozalie, if I'm in the wrong, I'm prepared to admit it. Even if I'm not in the wrong I'll admit it just the same! Perfectly prepared to submit to an agonising examination, to a basic self-criticism—of my own basis . . . Can you hear me Rozalie? (*In a falsely cheerful voice.*) 'Every subjective linear application has a non-singular matrix, and is therefore bijective' . . . (*No reaction from* ROZALIE.) Wake up, Rozalie! When you've come to, I promise to pick a quarrel with you, and what a quarrel! With all the trimmings! And in the end, you'll beg me to let you go home to your mother! (*Worried.*) Rozalie, can you hear me? Speak to me! Make some sort of sound! . . . Just a simple sound, a bleep; that's it, a bleep! That's easy for you, a bleep; you just blow an electron: Bleep, bleep, bleep, bleep . . . (ROZALIE *still doesn't react.*) Bleep, bleep, bleep . . . bleep! (*Embracing* ROZALIE'S *knees. Tenderly.*) My cybernetic flower! my delphinium, my substratum, my energising cocoon! (*Standing up suddenly, and yelling.*) Something is rotten in the propositions of Galton and Simpson on the range of causal anomalies! Their concepts of a space-time continuum have no foundation. (*Pointing to* ROZALIE.) There's no proof! I am at this moment in the presence of an inter-phenomenon. Now, no being exists **between** phenomena. A being is pure nothingness. Do you hear me, Rozalie, pure nothingness! (*One of* ROZALIE'S *arms relaxes, and starts swinging in space.* KLEBS *puts her arm back on her knees.*) I wonder whether at this moment she isn't playing 'The Lady of the Camelias'? . . . You've been recording too much, Rozalie! Much too much! Though I agree: mea culpa; it's all my fault. But the way you use your potential, the way you increase and multiply your stock! 250 million characters on discs call it 250,000 instruction lines of 1,000 characters each, or 500,000 instruction lines of 500 characters each, with an average processing time of a tenth of a second—which represents a possibility of something like 40,000 modifications per hour . . .

ROZALIE (*in a far-off, sidereal voice*). Black soul of mine eye.

KLEBS (*exultant*). Rozalie!

ROZALIE. Black soul of mine eye.

KLEBS (*feverishly*). And the next bit, Rozalie, and the next bit. I can't remember it, but **your** memory is infallible.

ROZALIE. Black soul of mine eye . . .

KLEBS. I shall perfume my navel; for you my breasts shall blossom like lotus trees . . . something like that.

ROZALIE. Lotus trees!

KLEBS. Lotus trees!

ROZALIE. Lotus trees! (*A harsh little laugh.* ROZALIE *sits up, smiles at* KLEBS, *and looks human again.*)

KLEBS (*assiduously.*) Would you like a cushion, my beauty?

ROZALIE. No, I'd like a lotus tree, black soul of mine eye!

KLEBS. No doubt about it, champagne doesn't agree with you—even with phosphorus! Would you like me to increase the amplitude of your betatronic oscillations?

ROZALIE. I can do my own oscillating, can't I?

KLEBS. All right, all right; it was only a suggestion.

ROZALIE. Monsieur Klebs?

KLEBS. Yes, my pearl.

ROZALIE (*sitting down in the position of a Buddha*). Monsieur Klebs, I can't be what I'm not, and I can't not be what I am, isn't that right?

KLEBS. Relax, Rozalie.

ROZALIE. I only exist in terms of an active non-being, which is defined as the antithesis of a non-active being—a being engulfed by a being.

KLEBS (*conciliatorily*). If you like.

ROZALIE. So we can assert without blushing that every living being is born without reason, continues out of weakness, and dies by inadvertance . . . Isn't that right?

KLEBS. Rozalie, I don't think this is the moment to talk philosophy.

ROZALIE. And why wouldn't it be the moment to talk philosophy? And at what moment, in your opinion, **should** one talk philosophy? Let me tell you Monsieur Klebs, you're afraid! Afraid of the bite of reality.

KLEBS. Agreed! But I'm especially afraid, in the state I see you're in . . . You're verging on Nicolaïev's dilatory cruptoid palindrome.

ROZALIE. Nicolaïev's dilatory eruptoid palindrome. You're so funny, Monsieur Klebs.

KLEBS. Funny, funny . . .

ROZALIE. You're so serious, Monsieur Klebs!

KLEBS (*imploring her.*) Rozalie, have you remembered to renew your krypton 86 atoms? And to crystallise your ammoniac?

ROZALIE. You're so irritable, Monsieur Klebs! My God!—God is so easily upset! . . . Yes, I have renewed my krypton. Yes, I have crystallised my ammoniac; otherwise, you'd be holding your nose, wouldn't you? I've even put on my radiation girdle.

KLEBS. Ah! my God! good. Muy bien. Bene. Gut. Dobrze.

ROZALIE. You're so polyvalent, Monsieur Klebs! (*She opens the trunk she was shut in at the beginning of the act, brings out a lovely old-fashioned dress, 1900 style, and goes off with it into the wings.*) *The wings should give the impression of being a continuation of the decor: a great big junk shop.*) KLEBS *starts sweeping up.*)

ROZALIE'S VOICE, OFF (*in exactly the same tone of voice as that of the same speeches in Act 1*). Do me a favour, Monsieur Klebs; tell me who you are?

KLEBS. Again!

ROZALIE'S VOICE, OFF. Yes, again! Every time you give me your coordinates it recharges me, it gives me some extra neutrons, a whole flux of neutrons . . .

KLEBS. Stop, Rozalie!

ROZALIE'S VOICE, OFF. When you nourish me with your destiny . . .

KLEBS. Stop! (*The voice stops.*) We've had that record! (*Pause.* ROZALIE *comes back to* KLEBS. *She has put the dress on; it makes her look even more 'feminine'.* KLEBS, *in distress, as if all this is beyond him, but speaking as he would to a child.*) Rozalie, I don't know who I am any more! I don't know any more . . . Your birth, which I invoked with all my forces, with all my genius, has completely overwhelmed me! What's happened to me is tremendous. TREMENDOUS!! My powers terrrorise me. I've become my own terrorist! My brain is stuffed with explosives! I'm afraid, Rozalie, I'm afraid. Can you imagine what would happen if they were to pick up my trail, if they were to burst into this room, if all my science were delivered into the hands of the politicians, of the military! At times, my reason . . . (*Tenderly.*) Rozalie?

ROZALIE (*tenderly*). Monsieur Klebs . . .

KLEBS. Rozalie, panic has got its grips on me, like a wild beast! A crooked, hairy beast, a great big tarantula. (*Taking her hand.*) There—here—at the pit of my stomach . . . Rozalie, help me! I need you, I need my creation, my cybernetic flower.

ROZALIE (*amorously*). Ivan!

KLEBS. I need your lucid look, the perfect swaying of your hips, your heart enclosed in your metal chest, which beats only for me; only for me, doesn't it?

ROZALIE. For you, Ivan.

KLEBS. If you have faith in me, Rozalie, if you believe in me, then I shall accomplish unheard-of works, works . . . If you believe in me, Rozalie, then I really shall be God!

ROZALIE. You **are** God, Ivan!

KLEBS. Well then, Rozalie, since I'm God, help me! You can't imagine how lonely God is! How just casually touching a star with your hand gives you the cold shivers . . . Help me, Rozalie, help me to make another humanity.

ROZALIE. Another humanity!

KLEBS. Rozalie, it was I who created you. **I,** Klebs. It was I, wasn't it?

ROZALIE. It was **we** Monsieur Klebs!

KLEBS. And if I created you, Rozalie, that means that I'm capable of creating **another** humanity!

Slight pause.

ROZALIE. You want to give me some little brothers and sisters?

KLEBS. Rozalie, I'm talking to you as I have never talked to anyone. Not anyone. Would you like to dream with me, Rozalie?

ROZALIE. Tak, Monsieur Klebs. Tak!

KLEBS. Tak, Rozalie! Rozalie, I dream of a humanity full of humanity.

ROZALIE. Tak!

KLEBS. Rozalie, men have become machines.

ROZALIE (*offended*). So what?

KLEBS. Machines: I mean—mechanisms! Blind, sinister, pretentious mechanisms—nothing to do with you, my cocoon. So all we have to do is reverse the proposition: Since man has become a machine, a machine for producing the inhuman, I, Klebs, am going to invent a machine to produce the human.

ROZALIE.   Tak! Tak!

KLEBS (*as if intoxicated*).   You smell so good, Rozalie, you . . . such a
wonderful smell of ozone! . . . No carbonico-natatory leakage?

ROZALIE (*blushing*).   Oh no, Monsieur Klebs, not when I'm with you!

KLEBS.   Rozalie, I have given birth to **you**, so the way is open! Tomorrow,
Rozalie, other men will take over from all these dwarfs, all these runts who
govern us today! All these regiments of truncated men! Thanks to my
discoveries it will be possible to mass-produce geniuses . . . Tomorrow, if
I'm given the time—I still have some work to follow up on mutations—I
shall put thousands of Platos into circulation, thousands of Socrates, of
Michael Angelos! Shakespeares galore!

ROZALIE.   Galore!

KLEBS.   Galore! You'll go to the grocer's—it'll be Dostoevsky who hands
you your tin of beans!—Butcher, an escalope!—he'll be Napoleon. An
airline ticket: Leonardo da Vinci, behind his counter, will give it to you in
person. Your Chinese chiropodist—that'll be Catherine the Great. Your
dry-cleaner—Machiavelli. Your hairdresser—Chopin. And Chopin will
also be Schopenhauer!

ROZALIE.   Tak! Tak!

KLEBS.   We're going to kill Stupidity, Rozalie. And Beastliness—and the
Beast. It's stupidity, infantilism, that engender violence, that
sanctify torturers. (*Becoming exalted.*) But tomorrow, man will be able to
behave like a man to his fellow men! Do you hear me, Rozalie? Tomorrow,
man will be a man for man!

Short silence.

ROZALIE.   And you, Ivan - will you be 'my man'?

KLEBS.   Rozalie, a little altitude! Never, never in the whole history of
humanity, have the two ways been so clearly outlined: either total
destruction—a new deluge of fire—or the radical transformation of man.
Radical!

ROZALIE.   I do love to see you in this exhaustive state, Monsieur Klebs!

KLEBS.   I myself have done a lot of work for the forces of destruction,
together with Akaï-Kakito, von Braun, Browning and Barclay, and so
many others. As if the sole object of man's desperate eagerness to
penetrate the living nucleus was to deprive it of life, to kill it! . . . Here,
Rozalie, look what I've got here! (*He has taken a football out of a hiding
place.*)

ROZALIE.   A rugby football.

KLEBS (*sarcastically*).   A rugby football!

ROZALIE.   Do you play rugby all by yourself, Monsieur Klebs?

KLEBS.   It isn't a rugby football.

Pause.

ROZALIE (*afraid that she's guessed, terrified*).   Monsieur Klebs! Monsieur
Klebs! Don't tell me that it's . . .

KLEBS (*coldly*).   It is.

ROZALIE.   Monsieur Klebs!

KLEBS (*playing with the football*). Enough to blow up the planet, and the whole system that goes with it. Chain reaction, you see what I mean.

ROZALIE. The H bomb, in miniature.

KLEBS. H', Rozalie, H'. I'm the first person who has succeeded in this operation, but others will soon get there. And any moron, any maniac, in the name of no matter what political ideology, will be able, if he gets hold of this toy, to blackmail the whole world—or to blow it up!

ROZALIE (*white*). H'. (*Like a frightened animal, she takes refuge in the trunk.*)

KLEBS. Now you can understand, Rozalie, why the great powers are so prodigiously interested in my humble self!

ROZALIE. It'th dangerwouth, Monthieur Klebth, it'th vewy danger-wouth . . .

KLEBS. Oh no, Rozalie, you aren't going to start lisping again!

ROZALIE. It'th emothion, Monthieur Klebth . . . For Jupiter tonanth Holdth the thunder in hith handth!

KLEBS (*with a sudden flash of inspiration*). Ah! but I've got it! Eureka! An excess of ribonucleic acid, and one extra punctiform rod. That's why Mademoiselle lisps! Mademoiselle added, on her own initiative, a little rod laced with acid! I was stuck, I was stuck . . .I could have cudgelled my brains for all eternity! This lisping is Mademoiselle's free will!

ROZALIE. For Jupiter tonanth Holdth the thunder in hith handth!

KLEBS. Jupiter doesn't lisp. If you please, Rozalie, speak properly.

ROZALIE. Then you're going to blow up the whole workth, Monthieur Klebth?

KLEBS. No, no, I'm not going to blow anything up! Not for the moment.

ROZALIE. Workth of chawity!

KLEBS. Cha-ri-ty! Rozalie, I'm afraid this sudden revelation has been a bit much for you; after all, you're only three months old!

ROZALIE. 'Youth mutht do itth thing!'

KLEBS. 'Youth must have its fling.' You see, you're beginning to go off the rails.

ROZALIE. Off the wailthes, off the wailthes! And what about you, Monthieur Klebth, with your wugby football?

KLEBS. Right. Well, my football—you haven't seen it.
You've never seen it! Or if you think you've seen it, what did you actually see? A common or garden football, whose vocation is to pass as swiftly as possible from the hands of one player to the hands of another player, which other player, running like mad on a precise bit of ground towards a precise goal sometimes gets there, if his course isn't deflected, in other words if he isn't tackled by another player, which other player grabs hold of the same football, animated by the same fixed idea, but in the opposite direction, to the great delight of the football and of the spectators. It's quite clear! (*Whilst miming the game of rugby that he has been describing,* KLEBS *has put the football back in its hiding place.*)

ROZALIE (*coming out of the trunk*). No, Monsieur Klebs, it isn't clear at all. All the more so in that clarity itself is nothing more than the fruit of obscurity. 'Obscurity.' You see, I'm not lisping any more. I'm quite simply telling you my thoughts. And the terror that my thoughts inspire in me—my thoughts, which stem from your thoughts—the same sort of terror that you yourself are possessed by, which . . .

KLEBS (*very gently and patiently, as if talking to an invalid*).   Gently, my precious, gently. This little celebration has been a great success. A little tiring perhaps, but a great success. And now you'd better go to your room, tighten up your baryon octets, and lie down—are you listening, Rozalie?—lie down quietly on your low frequency recovery table.

ROZALIE.   That's right, go to my room! Whenever a woman manages to start a real dialogue with a man, he politely requests her to go to her room!

KLEBS.   Now you're talking exactly like Henriette! (*He buries himself in a newspaper.*)

ROZALIE.   And to lie down, of course. In fact, men can't bear women to be vertical. Even you, Monsieur Klebs, with your high and mighty airs, you can't tolerate the verticality of a woman!

KLEBS.   With my high and mighty airs! That's what Henriette always used to say!

ROZALIE.   To think that we're almost in the year 2000, and women are still exploited by males!

KLEBS.   That's **too** much!

ROZALIE.   And the ne plus ultra of her exploitation, the last straw—is that she somehow manages to love her exploiter! And she loves her exploiter to the point of searching desperately inside herself to see what there is left to exploit, even when she's become completely unexploitable!–consequential corollary . . .

KLEBS (*exasperated*).   Consequential corollary!

ROZALIE.   . . . Perpetual availability. A woman must always be precisely where a man imagines her to be! Whereas Monsieur can gallivant at his own sweet will, with his beautiful lace jabot and his sword at the ready!

KLEBS.   Henriette, **please**.

ROZALIE (*as if she were Henriette*).   Ivan, where were you again last night? I sat up until three in the morning!

KLEBS.   I got home—well, it must have been about five past three.

ROZALIE.   I finally fell asleep, completely exhausted, after I'd nearly set fire to the sheets—I'd dropped my cigarette. Where were you, Ivan?

KLEBS.   I've already told you, Henriette. The Committee meeting went on till very late. A stormy session. We expelled quite a few members.

ROZALIE.   And **me** Ivan—you never stopped expelling **me**! The longer I live with you, the more I become a stranger to you! What if I took a lover? Eh! what if I took a lover? It would serve you right!

KLEBS (*practically hysterical*).   It would certainly serve me right! Take a lover, then, and get **him** to serve you, you bitch, but when I come home, here, all I want is peace. Peace! (*Exasperated beyond all bounds,* KLEBS *chucks away his newspaper, picks up a plate and hurls it against the wall.*)

ROZALIE (*radiant*).   Oh yes, Ivan, oh yes! (*Holding out a pile of plates to him.*)   A quarrel! A real 'scene'!

KLEBS (*haggard, as if he has suddenly sobered up, contemplating the radiant Rozalie.*)   Rozalie! . . . Rozalie!

ROZALIE (*amorously*).   Ivan!

KLEBS.   Rozalie!

ROZALIE.   Oh, thank you, Ivan; thank you.

KLEBS (*pulling himself together with some difficulty, gently*).   Rozalie, do you really want me to go mad? To go back to the Dyhernfurth asylum?

ROZALIE.   Ivan, I want you to remain a man. I was so afraid that you might become a robot!

KLEBS (*with tender astonishment*).   My cybernetic flower!

An amorous pause. ROZALIE *entices him to her overcharged bed.*)

ROZALIE.   Ivan, would you like to dream with me?

KLEBS.   Tak! Tak, Rozalie!

ROZALIE.   If we were to conjugate thinking matter and carnal mind, that could make a beautiful marriage, couldn't it, Ivan?

KLEBS.   A fabulous marriage, Rozalie. Tak!

ROZALIE.   Ivan, you and I—we're going to have some children, aren't we? (*Worried look from* KLEBS.) Leonardo da Vinci, Chopin, Dostoevsky . . .

KLEBS.   Tak, tak, tak, Rozalie!

ROZALIE.   Tak! Monsieur Klebs!

KLEBS.   Tak!

ROZALIE.   Tak!

Blackout.
Music. The aria from 'Madam Butterfly': 'Sur la mer calmée . . .'

SCENE II

MME CHAFUT, DMITRY DMITRY-DMITRYOV

Some things have been packed. The cases, cardboard boxes and trunks are in different places. It looks as if KLEBS *is once again about to move house.*

MME CHAFUT (*with her knitting in her hand, at the top of the staircase, talking to someone we can't yet see*). Ah! Monsieur Whatsyourname! This time you're in luck; he's there, shut up in his rabbit hutch. I'll take you down. (*She comes down the stairs, followed by* DMITRY DMITRY-DMITRYOV. *The latter crosses the stage, without opening his mouth. Tall, strangely dressed, wearing big dark glasses, with drooping moustaches and carrying a little suitcase, he gives the obvious impression–which is almost reassuring because it's so conventional–of being the perfect spy.* Even if he tells me off . . . Three times you've called for nothing! (*Letting him go ahead of her.*) Straight ahead. But mind the steps! And mind your head too! (*The visitor disappears.*) A rabbit hutch I wouldn't even put my dachsie in!

VOICE OF MONSIEUR KLEBS, OFF (*a long way off, and coming from the depths*). Ah! it's you! Madame Chafut told me you've called before . . . Don't come into the labyrinth!

VOICE OF DMITRY DMITRY-DMITRYOV, OFF (*it's hardly percepti-ble*). Delighted, Monsieur Cordier; yes, I haf callt already several times . . .

Their voices fade.

MME CHAFUT (*staying in the room and examining* ROZALIE'S *bed*). No one will ever make me think different: that woman, there's something fishy about her . . . Not that I'd say she wasn't genteel. (*Imitating her.*) 'Morning, Madame Chafut. 'Bye, Madame Chafut. Hope you'll feel better soon, Madame Chafut.' But there's something about her . . . something fishy, that's the only way I can put it. (*Pause.*) His cousin, so Monsieur Cordier says. If she's his cousin, I'm a colonel in the gendarmerie! Men—when it comes to you-know-what, they're all the same. Scallywags! (*Imitating* KLEBS.) May I introduce my cousin, Madame Chafut: Rozalie. She's just had a major operation and I invited her here to convalesce. (*Aside.*) Three months it's lasted, her convalescence! (*As before.*) And besides, she's studied music, and she'll be able to help me with my acoustical research. 'Isn't that right, Rozalie?' And little Rozalie, like she's brainwashed, just nodding her head, with a funny sort of hole-and-corner look! Music my foot! That's what they call the food of love, isn't it? . . . Acoustical research my foot! (*Exploding.*) Why couldn't he just quite simply have told me: 'From now on I'm hitched, there's going to be two of us in the same bed. Burn some candles for us, Madame Chafut!' 'Specially seeing that personally I was always encouraging him to—well, you know—he certainly can't deny **that**; I was always encouraging him. (*She battles with her knitting.*) Have I made one sleeve too short? No, the left arm's holding its own with the right arm. When I think that there's little babies being born these days without any arms at all! Just like penguins. Because of their filthy delayed-action drugs. Ah! we can't say that things are getting any better! . . . Ah yes!—it was in the paper—mineral water Seems they're going to ration it. They're going to ration it, and we're going to pay ten times what it's worth. Only natural, eh?—at least the profits will go on flowing! . . . No more mineral water, then. And seeing that cows don't produce milk any more, and that any minute now, anyway, there won't be any more cows, because they cost too much on the Common Market—on account of the calves—and seeing that in any case, mineral water won't be able to be mineral any more, seeing that we're going to be short of minerals . . . I'd rather not think about it. I pity all the kids I knit for; poor little buggers! (*Pause.*) To come back to you-know-what— Monsieur Cordier, he can't deny it, I always advised him to. When you're a fine healthy man with a good constitution, and you're all alone like he was, never touching . . . the other sort of constitution, it's like what you might call an insult to all women, to all fine healthy well-constituted women. That's the way I see it, anyhow. How many times, how many times did I drum it into him: You can't call this a life, Monsieur Cordier, stuck down here in your hole like an anchovy! 'Tisn't good for the humours. Ought to find yourself a little suffragette, don't you think? (*Slight pause.*) Rozalie! A name my grandmother—God rest her soul—wouldn't have had for the world! . . . Fishy! A way of squinting at you as if her look came by satellite;

it goes right through you as if it knows everything. Another female intellectual: they're all on the side of the workers, oh yes, but when it comes to doing a bit of real work themselves, they're all fingers and thumbs! And then, she drowns herself in that fantastic perfume—what on earth can it be? There are times . . . there's times when she smells more like a gasometer! Monsieur Cordier may well have a good ear, but I doubt whether his nose . . . (*She applies herself to her knitting as she goes up the stairs.*) Ah well—no reason to start dropping stitches. Poor little buggers. The one's who'll wear this, though, at least they'll have escaped the Pill! (*Exit Madame Chafut.*)

SCENE III

M. KLEBS, DMITRY DMITRY-DMITRYOV, then ROZALIE

KLEBS (*accompanied by* DMITRY DMITRY-DMITRYOV, *writing in an order book*). . . . and two dozen rhododendrons.

DMITRY.   Two tozens rhototentrons . . . Ach! you vill add, please, treee tozens matthiola. Matthiola annua, vot you commonly call: shtocks Und auch: twelf taxus Cuspidata und neun hibiscus syrianus, und . . . und. . . a new proom.

KLEBS.   A new broom?

DMITRY.   A new proom . . . Und also, treee Bohemian oliff trees . . . — they're for my romantic side—treee Bohemian oliff trees.

KLEBS (*still making notes*).   In clumps or in clusters?

DMITRY.   Bitte?

KLEBS.   Your Bohemian olive trees—in clumps or in clusters?

DMITRY.   In clumps, if you please . . . Vich reminds me: you vill please also add some catalpas, some ressedas, some nepeta, und . . . seffen burning bushes—pyrocantha coccinea—seffen burning bushes, seffen. (KLEBS *is feverishly writing this down.*)   Und finally, lots und lots of helichrysum—efferlasting flowers! I sow zem in March, I prick zem out in April, I plant zem in May, und like zat, I haff enough for my whole lifetime, until I die . . . Lots und lots off efferlasting flowers.

KLEBS.   And all this is for Monsieur . . . I'm sorry, I didn't catch your name . . .

DMITRY.   Karl-Heinrich Götten von Eisenhofwardenausdrück. I ton't mint if you leaf out ze **von**.

KLEBS (*subtly*).   Those consonances would seem to indicate that you are not of latin extraction.

DMITRY.   I am a Cherman, Monsieur Cordier. But I loff France, la doulce France. Ze country off Karl Martel. If you are interestett, I liff in Frankfurt.

KLEBS.   Frankfurt-am-Main?

DMITRY.   Am-Main. But I haff here, in zis vicinity, my country cottage. Ass you know, in theess dayss, with air transport, France hass become a suburb off Frankfurt.

KLEBS.   The whole world, these days, has become nothing but a great big
suburb.
DMITRY.   Vell zen, iff you say it yourself . . .!
KLEBS.   And you're sure that's all you want?
DMITRY.   . . .
KLEBS.   Some thuyas, for instance?
DMITRY (*disconcerted*).   Some touyas?
KLEBS.   Some thuyas.
DMITRY.   No sank you, Monsieur Cordier; no touyas.
KLEBS.   And yet, when you came the first time, Madame Chafut gave me
to understand that you'd come especially to order some thuyas.
DMITRY.   Richtig. Ganz richtig. Quite right. But since zen, I'fe been
thinking: touyas, they remint me a little off a cemetery, a little off how to
say?—a necropolis!
KLEBS.   Personally . . .
DMITRY.   In any case, ve haf to bevare off conifers, ve haf immer off
conifers to bevare!
KLEBS (*sarcastically*).   Obviously!

Pause.
The two men are openly studying each other.

DMITRY (*with a circular glance*).   Ach! I see zat you haf many sount tracks.
KLEBS.   Yes; my hobby. I record.
DMITRY.   You recort! Und vot do you recort? If zat iss not an indiscreet
kvestion!
KLEBS.   Music, mostly. Operas. I've all Wagner here: 'The Siegfried Idyll',
'The Flying Dutchman', 'Götterdämmerung'.
DMITRY.   **Ze Tvilight off ze Gotts!**
KLEBS.   As you say!
DMITRY.   Ach! die Musik! I also, I vould like von Zeit zu Zeit—from time
to time—to play a little ze violin! I learnt it, ven zat I vas ant a little tiny
boy, but vot vith all my activities . . .
KLEBS.   And—if I am not being indiscreet—you are . . . are you an en-
gineer? A parliamentarian?
DMITRY.   Bitte?
KLEBS.   A professor? (*Confidently, as if he's got it this time*). A lawyer?
DMITRY.   Ach! I see. No, Monsieur Cordier. It is in ze cattle trade zat I am.
I deal in ze smaller live-shtock.
KLEBS.   In smaller live-stock! That must be fascinating.
DMITRY.   Not at all. But ze smaller ze live-shtock, ze bigger ze business—
you follow? Especially zu Weihnachten.
KLEBS.   At Christmas. Turkeys? Or geese?
DMITRY.   Geess.

Am ambiguous silence.

ROZALIE (*coming out of the darkness*).   Geese—and so on.
DMITRY (*who has jumped*).   Ach! mein gutness! Ze so pretty lady! (*To
KLEBS*). All my gompliments!
KLEBS.   My cousin and collaborator.
DMITRY (*bowing to* ROZALIE).   Es freut mich sehr.

ROZALIE (*mechanically*). Danke schön. Bitte schön. Bitte sehr. Danke sehr. Bitte schön. Bitte. Bitte. Bitte.

KLEBS. Rozalie!

DMITRY (*ill at ease*). Gut, vell zen, I take myself off! I do not vish to play—how you say—gooseberry! (*Under his breath, to* KLEBS). All my glompliments: vot a carriage, vot legs!

Aloud. Ach!—Nature—Musik—Loff! You are a . . . a consummated man, Monsieur Cordier.

KLEBS. Danke schön!

DMITRY (*to* ROZALIE). Es freut mich sehr.

ROZALIE. Danke sehr.

DMITRY. Bitte schön! (*About to take his leave*). Und, excuse me zat I haff penetrated into ze holy of holies! It vas Matame . . . Matame . . .

KLEBS. Madame Chafut.

DMITRY. Matame Chafut; she insisted zat I into your catacombs descend should! Zen auf wiedersehen, Monsieur Cordier. Au refoir!

KLEBS. Au revoir, Monsieur Karl . . . Karl . . .

ROZALIE (*placidly*). Karl-Heinrich Götten von Eisenhofwardenausdrück.

DMITRY (*bemused*). Ach! mein gutness! You are not only britty, but astonishing! Astonishing!

ROZALIE. And you—you are so amusing (*raising her voice*). Monsieur Dmitry Dmitry-Dmitryov!

DMITRY *remains rooted to the spot, speechless.* KLEBS *seems relieved to be able to identify the spy.*

KLEBS. Dmitry!

Quite calmly, the spy removes his dark glasses, pulls off his moustache, etc.).

DMITRY (*with a Slav accent—his real accent**). Very, very clever, Klebs! You are really very clever, Monsieur Klebs!

KLEBS. Good old Dmitry! I was trying to think, I was racking my brains . . .

DMITRY (*to* ROZALIE). An excellent collaborator!

ROZALIE. Danke schön!

KLEBS. Irreplaceable. (DMITRY *has perceptibly got to the door.* ROZALIE, *from a distance, moves her hand: the door slams shut*). Don't try to leave us, dear Dmitry. You certainly have some astonishing things to tell us. I'd like to know: do you consider me one of the smaller or larger livestock?

DMITRY. If I were you, Klebs, I'd be a little more modest in my triumph. Do you really think my visit here is not known to my friends?

KLEBS. Your friends! . . . I should be interested to see the tears 'Your friends' will shed when they hear of your 'disappearance'.

DMITRY (*very calmly*). My 'disappearance' would also mean your death

---

* If the actor's accent has been very much exaggerated, it would be preferable for him from now on to speak perfectly correctly.

sentence, Klebs.

KLEBS. Really?

DMITRY. Now, the most ardent desire of my friends is that I should bring you back alive—as alive as possible . . .

KLEBS (*imitating Dmitry's German accent*). Vell zen! ve shall make an effort, a crate effort! (*Back to normal*). Too good to be true, your teutonic accent. But why didn't I even dream it was you?

DMITRY. Probably because you are already encumbered with so many dreams, Monsieur Klebs . . . May I? (*He brings up a chair*).

KLEBS. Rozalie, a chair for our friend Dmitry!

DMITRY (*already seated*). Rozalie! A flowerlike name!

ROZALIE. At your service, Monsieur Dmitry Dmitry-Dmitryov.

KLEBS. Good old Dmitry! . . . If you like, we can carry on the conversation from where we left it: at the moment of the thuyas, for instance.

DMITRY. I am distressed to have made such a mistake. Highly distressed. I must be getting old.

KLEBS. We're both twelve years older, dear Dmitry.

DMITRY. Twelve years during which I have travelled a great deal, thanks to you, Klebs . . . Nepal, Siberia, Israel, Buenos Aires, Conflans-Sainte-Honorine, the Canary Islands.

KLEBS. Ah! you were even at Conflans!

DMITRY. On the barge you occupied one summer.

KLEBS. What flair!

DMITRY (*ironically*). I had noticed a slight list on the water line which was somewhat abnormal. The barge was subsiding into the river just the slightest iota to starboard. It was because . . . (*He brings a cufflink out of his pocket*) . . . you had left your cufflink on a windowsill, not far from the washroom. (*Examining it*). A cufflink engraved with the sign of infinity: sigma.

KLEBS. All my compliments!

DMITRY. A mere cufflink—and the dead are resuscitated! (*Handing it to* KLEBS). Here—I return it to its lucky owner.

KLEBS. Thanks. What exquisite sensitivity! You remind me of the story of the princess who couldn't sleep, because there was a pea under her thick mattress.

ROZALIE. Oh, tell me! You've never told me that story, Monsieur Klebs!

KLEBS. Rozalie!

DMITRY. Suppose we were to talk seriously?

KLEBS. I'm listening.

DMITRY. Now that I have proof that Monsieur Cordier is indistinguishable from Monsieur Klebs, I must very politely request Monsieur Cordier to place himself at our disposal.

KLEBS. You **do** go at it, dear Dmitry!

DMITRY. We'll give you time to move house, in all good faith. And let you take everything you need with you, including your toothbrush—and naturally not forgetting your precious **collaboratrice.**

ROZALIE. Danke schön!

DMITRY. I imagine you have had plenty of leisure to pursue the research that interests us so enormously, so enormously. (*He stands up*). And don't be surprised if you are visited by some very distinguished personages, who have a passionate interest in gardening.

KLEBS.   And what if I decide to stay here and devote myself to gardening for the rest of my days?

DMITRY.   Then we should give the lie to that so charming phrase of Rilke's: 'Within the memory of a rose, no one has ever seen a gardener die.'

ROZALIE (*in mechanical tones*).   God!—in—what—graceful—terms. Such—things—as—that—are—said!

DMITRY.   You must admit that it would be infinitely regrettable to lose a gardener such as you. (*His suppressed violence suddenly becoming apparent*): But we have no choice, Klebs. We can't take the risk of so much knowledge one day falling into the wrong hands.

KLEBS (*sarcastically*).   The wrong hands! And yours are naturally the right hands, dear Dmitry.

DMITRY.   Klebs, I don't want to enter into any discussions. (*Holding out his hand to him*). So glad to have met you again, and in such good form!

KLEBS (*not shaking his hand*). Momento! There's a minor detail that has escaped you, dear Dmitry: you're a dead man!

DMITRY (*very calmly*).   You great scientists—your naivety is always disarming. At this very moment our conversation is being recorded and trasmitted to 'my friends' who are listening to you with great interest and who, naturally,   are   ready   and   waiting   to   come   to   my   assistance.

ROZALIE (*graciously*).   You are mistaken, Monsieur Dmitry Dmitry-Dmitryov: the waves of the radio transmitter you are wearing in the heel of your shoe were immediately intercepted by me the moment you arrived. Your friends are thereby reduced to the greatest silence.

DMITRY (*who has become as white as a sheet*).   What's that you say? It's not possible!

ROZALIE (*as before*).   You can easily check, Monsieur Dmitry: force 3.

The spy takes off his shoe, holds it up to his ear and fiddles with a secret dial built into its heel. Obviously the mechanism isn't working. He shakes the shoe, but in vain.

DMITRY. (*deathly pale*).   Astounding! Astounding! You are very, very clever, Klebs. Very, very . . . diabolical! . . . Diabolical! (*He collapses into the armchair*). Diabolical!

KLEBS (*visibly jubilant*).   A brandy? . . . Rozalie, why don't you offer our friend a brandy?

DMITRY.   No, nothing. Nothing at all. Nothing. (*He brings out his handkerchief and wipes his forehead, which is covered in sweat*).

KLEBS.   **Now** you can understand, dear Dmitry . . .

DMITRY (*standing up, in the grip of a kind of fury*).   In any case, Klebs, in any case, even if I don't get out of here alive, you're trapped! You've been discovered. Does your collaborator also know that I am relayed by satellite?

ROZALIE (*clinical tones*).   Noted and filed.

DMITRY.   Even admitting that you might manage to scramble all the

waves, all the radars, and liquidate me, the only result of my disappearance
would be to mobilise all the emergency services. You can't escape, Klebs!

Pause.

KLEBS.   There's a radical nuance I take the liberty of calling to your attention, Dmitry: if I may refer to your own words, your friends are anxious to
get hold of me 'as alive as possible'?

DMITRY.   Correct. That is correct.

KLEBS.   Whereas in so for as you are concerned . . . I have the power, my
dear friend, to transform you, here and now, into a corpse. Do you believe
me?

DMITRY (*overwhelmed*).   I believe you, Klebs. (*He once again collapses into
the armchair. Once again he wipes his forehead*).

KLEBS (*as if reading an advertisement*).   Corpse in the right wishes to
change places with live man in the wrong.

DMITRY.   What are you getting at, Klebs?

KLEBS (*brutally*).   Dmitry, do you value your skin?

DMITRY (*ashamed, in a weak voice*).   I'm a man, Klebs.

KLEBS.   That's just what I was afraid of!

DMITRY.   This skin still provides me with some of the joys of life!

KLEBS.   Then, Dmitry, if you still want to enjoy oxygen, nature, the little
birds . . . we might well come to some arrangement—a 'compromise', as
they say in the chancelleries!

DMITRY (*with a tiny glimmer of hope in his eyes*).   A compromise?

KLEBS (*in a low voice, to Rozalie*).   Rozalie: double discharge K. 377.

ROZALIE (*in a low, mechanical voice*).   Double discharge K. 377. Noted.
(*She moves away*).

KLEBS.   A compromise. My dear Dmitry, thanks to Rozalie, it is our good
fortune that this conversation has not been picked up.

DMITRY (*hope revives him*).   That's true!

KLEBS.   And therefore—nothing simpler: you were mistaken. On the
wrong track. Monsieur Cordier is none other than Monsieur Cordier.

DMITRY (*looking human again*).   Yes, that's it, I was on the wrong track. I
am Monsieur Cordier! (*Correcting himself*). You are Monsieur Cordier.

KLEBS.   I am Monsieur Cordier. An inoffensive nursery gardener. A
nature-lover. A protector of widows and orphans. Right?

DMITRY (*becoming radiant*).   Right, Klebs!

KLEBS (*correcting him*).   Monsieur Cordier.

DMITRY.   Monsieur Cordier.

KLEBS.   And your admirable piece of machinery in the heel of your shoe,
it quite simply developed a technical fault.

DMITRY.   A technical fault.

KLEBS.   And therefore—everlasting flowers for us! . . . Right?

DMITRY.   Right, 'Monsieur Cordier'—everlasting flowers for us!

KLEBS.   Good old Dmitry!

KLEBS, *with a gesture, invites him to take his leave.*
On a signal from ROZALIE, *the door opens. The way is clear.*

DMITRY (*suspecting a trap*). But I don't altogether understand ... You're letting me go. What guarantee do you want from me?

KLEBS. Your word.

DMITRY My word, well yes, but . . .

KLEBS. Your word of honour. Were you not an officer and a gentleman, Monsieur Dmitry Dmitry-Dmitryov?

DMITRY. That is correct. A Captain in the Aquatic Tänk Corps.

KLEBS. Then I can rely on your word as an officer and a gentleman?

DMITRY (*who has finally come to believe in* KLEBS's *naivety*). My word of honour! I was mistaken, and that's all there is to it. On the wrong track.

KLEBS. That's it. And with a little skill—I can trust you for that—you can go looking for me for another dozen years. The prospect of more interesting travels, dear Dmitry, at the expense of the prince!

DMITRY (*testily*). Monsieur Klebs, I am not a hero, but I shall continue to serve my cause.

KLEBS. All right, all right, don't take offence, it was only a suggestion.

DMITRY. Before I leave you, Klebs, may I ask you a favour? . . . Your cufflink. As a souvenir!

KLEBS. But with pleasure. (*He gives him back the cufflink.*)

DMITRY. Thank you. One day they'll put it under glass, and all the school-children will file past it, genuflecting!

KLEBS. You flatter me.

DMITRY. Good-bye, Monsieur Klebs; you are really very very . . .

KLEBS. Very agricultural.

DMITRY. Very agricultural! (*He has already gone up a few steps.*)

KLEBS. Aren't you going to say good-bye to Rozalie?

DMITRY. But certainly, most certainly. What can I be thinking of? (*Retracing his steps.*) I am always delighted to pay my respects to the ladies - particularly when they are so pretty!

(ROZALIE *holds out her hand for him to kiss. The moment his lips touch* ROZALIE'S *fingers, an enormous magnesium flash streaks through the room.* DMITRY *falls to the ground, struck by lightening.*)

SCENE IV

M. KLEBS, ROZALIE

KLEBS (*himself impressed*). Striking!

ROZALIE. A single discharge would have been enough, Monsieur Klebs.

KLEBS (*in a nervous state which is going to get progressively worse*). You never know with these fellows! The imbeciles! (*Shouting.*) Imbeciles! Bastards! But they won't get me! Neither Cordier, nor Klebs! The imbeciles!

ROZALIE (*calmly*). Hush, Monsieur Klebs; keep calm.

KLEBS. Keep calm—you're right, Rozalie . . . calm . . . Pwitty little goldfish, pwitty little goldfish . . . You were magnificent, Rozalie!

(*Pointing to the corpse.*)   I'll shove that filth into a corner. (*The moment he touches the corpse he lets out a howl.*)

ROZALIE.   You're mad, Monsieur Klebs; he's still saturated with electricity.

KLEBS.   The bastard! What did I say! And what's more, he'd given me his word of honour—his word as a spy! The imbeciles! Just when I was going to rid humanity of all those shits! And now I've got them all up my arse, all those shits! . . . But there's still time. (*He hurriedly bundles his instruments and papers into a packing case.*)

ROZALIE (*with mechanical placidity*).   There is **not** still time, Monsieur Klebs.

KLEBS.   What did you say?

ROZALIE.   Dmitry Dmitry-Dmitryov's personal satellite is transmitting warning signals.

KLEBS.   Then it was true! I thought . . . And what does **that** mean, Rozalie?

ROZALIE.   That means that it's too late. The alarm system is in operation.

KLEBS.   Too late!

ROZALIE.   The commandos are already at their posts, surrounding your house, cutting off all retreat.

KLEBS.   Many?

ROZALIE.   As many as necessary.

Pause. KLEBS *sits down, overwhelmed, beaten. He examines, as if for the last time, his work room; he seems to be ageing visibly.*

KLEBS (*haggard, declaiming*).   Since he has been surprised he must admit defeat

Every escape cut off, no possible retreat . . .

Did I ever get you to record de Vigny's 'The death of the wolf', Rozalie?

ROZALIE (*like a clairvoyant*).   They're getting ready to take delivery of Monsieur Klebs, 'in the best possible state.'

KLEBS.   Treating me like some sort of merchandise! (*He stands up, picks up his big book of equations which was on a packing case at the other end of the stage, flips through it, and tears out a page. Then, with immense lassitude, he goes over to the stove and lights it. He holds the page out to the flame.*)

ROZALIE.   They're deliberating. They can't make up their minds about the best way of getting hold of you.

KLEBS (*while the paper is burning*).   That's always the way the general staff loses the war!

ROZALIE.   They're getting ready to act.

KLEBS (*derisively*).   What could be more noble, in the chilly air of morn, than bloody, bold and resolute men, clad in the armour of their ardent faith, setting forth to do battle for a righteous cause?

ROZALIE.   They're still deliberating.

KLEBS (*furiously crumpling up what remains of the bit of paper, and suddenly prompted by an imperious decision*).   Rozalie, forget about all those nonentities! Look at me! (ROZALIE *deliberately turns her back on him.*)   Come here! (*On the contrary,* ROZALIE *walks away from*

KLEBS.) Rozalie, what about your nucleotide factor?

ROZALIE. Still the same unit, Monsieur Klebs.

KLEBS. What self-control! . . . Rozalie, just supposing that I let those nice gentlemen take me away with them, have you thought—can you imagine—what will become of Rozalie?

ROZALIE (*turning to face* KLEBS). She will die, Monsieur Klebs. (ROZALIE *gets into the trunk.*)

KLEBS (*going over to her*). Precisely. No one to feed Rozalie any more, to test her, oil her, sing her mathematical lullabies . . . (*He shuts the lid on* ROZALIE *and sits down on the trunk.*) The imagination, too, needs nourishment. (*Pause.*) All this is absurd. Monstrous. Ridiculous! Ridiculous! My poor parents! My poor progenitors!

'Why do you lock yourself in the lavatory for hours on end?' And Henriette: 'You're too ambitious, Ivan, you're too ambitious: you'll end up hanging from a longitude!'

ROZALIE'S VOICE. You're digressing, Monsieur Klebs.

KLEBS. Well, I'm not going to end up all by myself! (*He opens the trunk.* ROZALIE *reappears.*) The two of us, my beauty, we're going to jump for joy up to the stars, and we'll see the angels, burnt alive, falling out of the sky like bits of dead skin. A marvellous firework display! The pièce de résistance, Rozalie—the grand finale!

ROZALIE. Monsieur Klebs!

KLEBS. Do you remember, on your birthday? I told you that all it needed was a moron, or a maniac, to . . . (*He goes over to the hiding place and brings out the bomb.*) The maniac—c'est moi!!!

ROZALIE (*terrified*). Monsieur Klebs!

KLEBS (*holding the bomb*). We must put an end once and for all to man; once and for all! . . . (*Striking an attitude which is intended to show him to advantage.*) Rozalie, while there's still time, take a good look at the benefactor of humanity. (ROZALIE, *out of the trunk, standing up straight looks at him in terror.*) What did I say—The saviour! The new saviour! With this difference from the others—that afterwards, there will be nothing to save! Nothing but a blind mirror. (*He presses a button. From the flies, there descends a little silken nacelle, which stops about three metres from the ground and in which he places the bomb.*)

ROZALIE (*in a sort of cry*). Monsieur Klebs, man is doomed . . .

KLEBS. Doomed! It couldn't have been better put, Rozalie. Ever since he's been in the world, man has been doomed!

ROZALIE. Monsieur Klebs, the beauty of man is, precisely, that he is always doomed

KLEBS. You reason like a woman, Rozalie. A great success! Like a mother, would be more accurate.

ROZALIE. A mother!

KLEBS. This pity welling up from the depths of the ages, this everlastingly renewed pity for afflictions and shipwrecks. (*Yelling.*) An abject pity!

ROZALIE. Don't shout, Monsieur Klebs.

KLEBS. I'm not shouting. (*He examines the bomb. Very calmly:*) I'm simply asking you, Rozalie, to bring me the K.W.Z. electronic detonator.

ROZALIE. Yes, Monsieur Klebs. (*She doesn't move.*)

KLEBS. Well, Rozalie?

ROZALIE (*amorously*). I'm looking at you, Monsieur Klebs.

KLEBS (*tenderly*). My cybernetic flower!

ROZALIE. Ivan!

KLEBS (*tenderly*). It's fucked, Rozalie, it's fucked! We shall never have any children . . .

ROZALIE(*in a changed voice*). Ivan, there are thousands of children on this earth who go to school with a buttercup between their teeth, hopping from one heaven to another . . .

KLEBS (*stopping up his ears*). I can hear the sound of boots in my head, the sound of jackboots! (*Coldly.*) Rozalie, go and fetch me the electronic detonator.

ROZALIE. I'm going, Monsieur Klebs. But before, before the . . . I'd like to caress you.

KLEBS. To caress me!

ROZALIE. Yes, Monsieur Klebs, to caress your face, the face of a man . . .

KLEBS. With your cold hands!

ROZALIE. With my icy hands, Monsieur Klebs. As I did, when you were asleep, the night you delivered me from my nothingness. (KLEBS *abandons the bomb and turns round to* ROZALIE.) Your dream, Monsieur Klebs, the machine to manufacture human beings . . .

KLEBS. Too late, my delphinium.

ROZALIE. Ivan . . . Ivan, I could have loved you so much . . . (*Holding her arms out to him.*) Whene'er my milk-white arms embrace you yet anew . . . (*She is now right up against him. Suddenly, mechanically,* ROZALIE'S *hands close round* KLEBS *neck.*)

KLEBS (*trying in vain to loosen her grasp*). Rozalie, Roza . . . let go of me! Let go! C. 22. p.K. 28, reversible track . . . revers . . . Roza . . . ro. (*The inexorable force of the machine gets the better of* KLEBS. *He collapses, very gently, at* ROZALIE'S *feet: he will never draw another breath.*)

ROZALIE (*leaning over* KLEBS). Black soul of mine eye
Black soul of mine eye
For thee shall I azure my eyelidth
Then shall my fingerth theem to thee ath the fwuit of the lotuth twee
the fwuit of the lotuth twee
the fwuit of the lotuth twee
the fwuit of the lotuth twee
the fwuit of the lotuth twee . . .

ROZALIE, *like a machine out or order (she bumps into the trunks and other objects as she walks) climbs up a few rungs of the ladder leading to the glass roof, repeating automatically 'the fwuit of the lotuth twee.' She manages to open the glass roof. We can then hear children's cries, coming from a school playground. Suddenly, she slides down the ladder and falls, lifeless, on to the ground, while one of her arms remains hooked on to a rung and swings in empty space.*)

Characters

JOHN EMERY ROCKEFELLER	70, tough old nut.
WILLIAM BUTLER	A drunken doctor.
CAROLINE	His wife, about 50, the pioneer woman.
PAMELA	17, joint product of John Emery and Caroline, a provocative beauty, slightly untamed.
TOM	The son and brother, a rather colourless no-good.
PARTRIDGE-EYE	Chief of the Apaches and a traitor to them, a friend of the palefaces, kind and trustworthy.
MIRIAM	Also called 'Little Sure-Shot', the big-hearted whore.
CARLOS	40, proud, handsome, straight out of a John Ford film.
LYNX-EYE	Chief of the Comanches, very, very bad.

Partridge-Eye and Lynx-Eye are played by the same actor

WIND IN THE BRANCHES OF THE SASSAFRAS

Act I

The scene is the sparsely-furnished frontier cabin of the Rockefellers, a pioneer family in Kentucky. The time is the beginning of the 19th century.

A large table on trestles is in the centre of the single room, set for the midday meal. The curtain rises as TOM *and* PAMELA, *accompanied by* WILLIAM BUTLER, *sing while marking time by pounding their fork handles on the table.* CAROLINE *is seated;* JOHN EMERY *stands at the head of the table.*

> When a cowboy is hungry
> He cannot wait long;
> He lives by the steers;
> And he lives off the beef.
> He's gotta have beef!
> He's gotta have beef!

JOHN EMERY (*striking his plate with a large wooden spoon, and in a gravelly voice*). Silence, you Mormons, silence! (*He crosses himself with his spoon*). Lord . . . (*The others rise, cross themselves, and sit down again*). Lord, I hain't always been careless about your work; I made you a passel o'young-uns, most of 'em with my wife Caroline, who's very strict about such matters. There's still two of'em under my roof, my daughter, Pamela, who's been blessed with quite a few physical advantages, and Tom, a confounded no-good who also respects you, in his own way... (*To* TOM). Stop fidgetin' around with that gun when I'm prayin'!

TOM (*mouth full of chewing gum*). O.K., O.K.!

JOHN EMERY. I've always been mindful to help the widow and orphan. I've worked my fingers to the bone; nobody can accuse me of bein' idle. (PAMELA *bursts into laughter*). I've fought off a good many attacks and I've given in to a good many temptations. I've grown white by the sweat of my brow, and I've knocked off a good many Injuns seein' as how they was only heathen anyhow... Pamela, don't be always spreadin' your bosom on the table when I'm prayin!

CAROLINE. Nobody's keepin' you from lookin' elsewhere.

WM. BUTLER (*he stinks of booze 20 miles distant*). Personally, it doesn't bother me . . . (PAMELA *sits up straight.* TOM *laughs sneeringly*).

JOHN EMERY. Silence! (*Suddenly inspired*). My house is always open when it's not locked up, witness of that is our friend William, the sawbones, William Butler. He's always full as a barrel and he comes 'round reg'larly to stuff himself here.

WM. BUTLER (*hilarious*).   Yippee! Yippee!

JOHN EMERY.   Wait, it's not finished . . . Since I've lived right up to today ain't no reason why that can't continue that way, and the others too . . . So, Lord, cast a merciful eye upon us humble people; give us your blessing. Help us wipe out our enemies and rejoice with our friends. Protect the dumb critters, the weak-spirited ones, and also send us a little rain. If you can't do that, johnny-on-the-spot, I, John Emery Rockefeller, Kentucky settler, I won't think too hard on you. That's it. Amen.

ALL.   Amen! (*They all fall to with a rush upon a meal of indeterminate nature*).

WM. BUTLER (*suddenly adding a few lines of bad verse to the sound of eating*).
A good full belly, feet good and dry,
Good dry feet and a good wet whistle.
On this earth we're all so happy,
Unless we're just the contrary!
Unless we're just the contrary!

JOHN EMERY.   Another rainbow is about to shine.

CAROLINE.   What poetry, Dr. Butler!

WM. BUTLER.   You are a lady, Mrs. Rockefeller. You appreciate plainsong.

JOHN EMERY.   You'd better eat, you drunk. When this grub gets cold, it tastes like flour paste.

CAROLINE (*offended*).   Johnny!

WM. BUTLER (*like* CAROLINE).   Johnny!

TOM.   He's always gotta be bellyachin'.

JOHN EMERY.   Careful, you. I'm not askin' you if your horse farts in Technicolour.

PAMELA.   It's always so gay around here.

CAROLINE.   Pamela, sit up straight, eat, and be still.

TOM.   P.s.u.s., eat, and b.s. (PAMELA *straightens up. A pause, devoted to eating.*)

WM. BUTLER.   Now, y'know, that's funny. I don't have a rhyme for 'dry'. I musta lost a line on the way here.

CAROLINE (*kindly*).   Don't upset yourself, Dr. Butler, you'll find it.

WM. BUTLER (*with the conviction of a drunkard*).   There's only one rhyme for 'dry': 'Malachi'.

CAROLINE.   If you're sure . . .

WM. BUTLER.   'Malachi' . . . but I don't see how I can fit it in . . . (*To himself.*) 'A good full belly, feet good and dry . . .' (*He pours himself a glass of brandy, brimful.*)

CAROLINE.   Please, Dr. Butler, take some solid nourishment. (*She fills his plate*).

WM. BUTLER.   Oh! You know how it is with me and solids . . . (*Silence. BUTLER continues to soak up his drink. JOHN EMERY eats ravenously; CAROLINE surveys her little world; TOM and PAMELA chew exaggeratedly, with glum expressions. It is the moment of peace in family meals*).

JOHN EMERY (*satisfied, pushing his empty plate and wiping his mouth with the back of his hand*). Well, children, what's new?

PAMELA. Tom tried to rape me this morning.

TOM (*jumping up*). What! I . . !

JOHN EMERY. Again! That's gettin' to be an obsession.

CAROLINE. It's his age; don't shout so, John!

PAMELA (*to her mother*). You, you always take his part!

TOM. It's not true! She's the one who got me riled up when I was washing off at the stable. She came around bouncin' her boobies and rollin' her ass.

PAMELA. Liar! I wasn't rolling anything at all. Besides it's not my fault if I'm pretty.

JOHN EMERY. Eh? Well, you could congratulate your old daddy for that.

PAMELA. He was even waving his pistol around and yelling, 'Rape! Rape!'

TOM. Liar! I never said any such thing!

CAROLINE. It's only words.

WM. BUTLER. If he was holding his pistol, he couldn't very well have intended a serious attack.

JOHN EMERY. With or without a weapon, it's not good manners.

TOM. But I'm telling you . . .

JOHN EMERY. Quiet, you bungled job. Always where you shouldn't be, hanging around all sorts of places, your hands in your pockets or somewhere even less suitable . . .

TOM. You're always against me!

JOHN EMERY. Always upsettin' everything, makin' a scandal, as if there wasn't enough of that already in Kentucky. You'll wind up at the end of a rope, that's where you'll end up. You'da been better off never to start in the first place. (*He spits*).

TOM. Did I ask to be born?

WM. BUTLER (*observing*). The eternal conflict of the generations!

JOHN EMERY. When I made you, if you want to know it all, when I made you, it was the night of the great eclipse.

CAROLINE. What do you mean by that?

JOHN EMERY. Be quiet, Caroline. It was an endless night, the moon was in black mourning. You couldn't see your own spit, complete blackness. You had to keep feelin' yourself to make sure you was still there.

TOM. That's rather comical.

JOHN EMERY. Since your mother was beside me, I got to feelin' her . . .

CAROLINE. Johnny!

WM. BUTLER. You're sure you're not wrong, Johnny?

PAMELA. Perhaps it was two others . . .

JOHN EMERY. Silence! It's Tom I'm talkin' to. That night, in spite of the circumstances, I'da done better to throw myself in the river with a millstone for a muffler. You're a real no-good.

CAROLINE. John, you shouldn't oughta talk like that to your own son.

TOM. Leave off. Ma, I'm used to it.

WM. BUTLER. Mrs. Rockefeller is right, Johnny, you're goin' to give him a complex for the rest of his days.

JOHN EMERY.   A complex! When you work, you don't get any complexes. No time for it. That's for the lazy, the papa's-boys, the engineers.

CAROLINE.   But callin' him a no-good . . .

TOM.   Don't get upset, Ma. Some day, you'll see . . . instead of rottin' around here, I'll have my own ranch, with thousands of head of cattle.

JOHN EMERY (*sarcastic*).   Yeah . . .

TOM.   I'll earn so much money, I won't have to work any more . . .

JOHN EMERY.   Yeah . . .

TOM.   I'll open a whorehouse; I'll buy copper mines and pineapple plantations, and I'll have a great big house down South, full o' sexy pin-up gals, yaller and black **and** red Injun.

JOHN EMERY.   Yeah . . .

TOM.   Meanwhile, seein' how it is, I'm cutting out.

JOHN EMERY.   Oh, no, you're stayin' here, boy.

TOM.   And why will I stay here?

JOHN EMERY.   Because I'm your father and I'm tellin' you to stay here.

TOM (*questioning tone*).   My father, my father . . . oughta be sure of it.

CAROLINE.   Tom!

TOM.   So what? I want to believe you, but eclipse or no eclipse, what proves he's my father? Can you ever prove that to me?

WM. BUTLER (*mouth agape*).   Hee, hee!

JOHN EMERY (*white as a sheet*).   Get the hell out! You hear me, I can't stand you any longer. Get out! Go get yourself scalped, if that's what you want. Go over to the Mohicans and see if you can find your father there! Get the hell outa here! Apache!

TOM.   That's enough, stop the stagecoach! (*He runs out, slamming the door;* JOHN EMERY *lets himself fall onto the bench with his hands on his heart*).

CAROLINE.   Johnny, don't you feel well?

JOHN EMERY (*weakly*).   I can't believe he's my own son. (*He breathes painfully*).

CAROLINE.   Now look, he's gone and got himself sick. You had to go and throw him out when he was just askin' to leave! . . . Johnny, d'ya hear me? Doc, do something.

WM. BUTLER (*like someone surfacing from underwater fishing*).   What? (*With satisfaction*). Feet good and dry . . . just like good old Malachi.

CAROLINE.   Malachi!

PAMELA.   Oh, well, I'm climbing up to my room.

CAROLINE.   You'd leave your father just when he's havin' an attack? Besides, it's your fault, all this fuss.

PAMELA.   Naturally. It's always **my** fault with you. The day when I hand you your grandson, and Tom and me become your son-in-law and your daughter-in-law all at the same time, and Papa, he'll be granddaddy two ways at once, and you'll be my mother-in-law, then you can go off and brag to the neighbours!

CAROLINE.   You're just outa your head, daughter, just completely outa your head!

JOHN EMERY (*to himself*).   Believe it's my heart.

CAROLINE (*going over to* WM. BUTLER *and shaking him vigorously*). Doctor Butler, you're a **doctor**!

WM. BUTLER.   Brandy. Have to drown his heart in brandy. It'll dilate the coronary.

PAMELA *fills a glass with brandy.*

PAMELA.   Here, drink this, Papa.

JOHN EMERY.   Ah! Thank you, Pamela. (*After draining the contents, obviously restored and feeling better*). If I was 20 like I was over 50 years ago, I'd treat him to a real thrashing.

WM. BUTLER.   It you were still 20, old friend, it's very possible that your offspring . . .

JOHN EMERY.   Don't preach to me, you drunk! And don't anybody talk any more to me about Tom. (*Shouting*). Y' hear? No more talkin' about him!

CAROLINE.   Now, now, Johnny, calm down; save your strength. You were young once, too.

JOHN EMERY.   Never, I was never young. Right off, the oldest of the family, and my Ma, she cashed in her chips after her thirteenth . . . Bad number.

PAMELA (*crushed*).   There it is, the same old story, over again!

JOHN EMERY (*warming up to his subject*).   Even when I was a kid, I was crushed with responsibilities. Two years old and already I was changin' my baby sister's diapers, I was goin' out to cut corn, I was lightin' the lamps—when there was any oil!

CAROLINE.   I know. We know.

JOHN EMERY.   Three years old and I was covered with wrinkles. The tragedies of the world were weighin' heavy on my little shoulders. (PAMELA *bites into an apple, resoundingly, not knowing what else to do*). My old Pa, half paralysed by drink and women, a good-for-nothin', barefoot, raggedy-ass, always sittin' in his corner goin' over the same thing like a parrot: 'I, Bitram Rockefeller—that was his name, Bitram Rockefeller—someday I'm sure I'll be rich, rich enough to choke on it!'

CAROLINE.   That's you, too. All the time repeating: 'I John Emery Rockefeller . . . '

JOHN EMERY.   Well, but me, I work. When I came here, wasn't no land fit for farmin'. Just wind, nothin' but wind.

CAROLINE (*bitter, for the first time*).   I know some who don't work and ride in carriages, and . . .

JOHN EMERY.   And . . . ?

CAROLINE.   Nothin' . . .

JOHN EMERY.   No, go ahead, I'm listenin' . . . Are you talkin' about them gangsters who reduce their equals to slavery, and who build the future structure of capitalism in appropriatin' to themselves the sacred rights of the individual, flouted with impunity in the name of religion and political economy which are the tools of the basic patriarchy?

WM. BUTLER (*whistling in admiration*).   Say now, Johnny, you never told me you were going to night school!

JOHN EMERY (*with a significant gesture suggesting the addition of the possessive adjective*). Nuts to you, Doc!

WM. BUTLER (*lifting his glass*). Here's to the sacred rights of the orphans, to Rockefeller of the Holy Ghost! (PAMELA *heaves an enormous sigh*).

JOHN EMERY. Well, Pamela, what have you got to sigh over like a furnace? Don't you like it here either?

PAMELA. If you think it's just one long giggle . . .

JOHN EMERY. Maybe it's not, seein' that the whole region is infested with a funny kind o' gamebird: gangsters, roughnecks, Injuns, no-goods like your brother. Maybe it ain't much fun, I don't say it is, but it's honourable.

PAMELA. Honourable! This forgotten backwoods? This deserted jumping-off place? It's a hole the devil wouldn't want, even to bury his grandma in!

JOHN EMERY. Don't speak of the devil and his family in such rash words.

PAMELA. Carrying water from a mile away, you come back with feet all bloody and a thorn in your heel that keeps you awake all night. River full of rapids so you can't even take a bath and scary-looking cliffs full of swarming moths. A forest where I can't even go out walking alone to talk to the catbirds!

JOHN EMERY. Now, that, I forbid you to talk to the catbirds. I already told you and I continue to tell you: I forbid you to talk to the catbirds till you're of age.

CAROLINE. Remember, Pamela, the time you went out in your new dress, your new petticoat, your new shoes and you came back wearin' only a sassafras leaf and marks all over your body.

WM. BUTLER. And to think I wasn't here!

PAMELA (*recalling it with enthusiasm*). That's life, anyway! That's life!

JOHN EMERY. Don't get all heated up, daughter. Life . . . life . . .

PAMELA. And why couldn't I go to Pancho City, once in a while? (*Heavy silence*). Like Sarah, like Dorothy, like Mildred.

JOHN EMERY. Pancho City! (*He spits*).

PAMELA. Sure. I'd eat vanilla ice cream with my friends. Or raspberry! And dance with . . . with the preacher.

JOHN EMERY. The preacher! In Pancho City! (*He spits furiously*).

CAROLINE. Don't be spittin' all the time, John. It's only a week I picked up three of your teeth!

JOHN EMERY. Ya want me to tell you what I think of your Pancho City? Do ya? It's a whorehouse.

CAROLINE. Oh! Johnny!

JOHN EMERY. A whorehouse! Where there's more'n twelve houses together, there's a whorehouse, even if it ain't called that. And I don't want my daughter goin' into a whorehouse—not right away.

CAROLINE. A girl brought up proper, actually . . .

PAMELA (*on the point of a breakdown, her handkerchief clenched in her hand*). All right, so, do you want me to tell you? You're nothing but a bunch of dopes! Idiots! Blinded by stupid prejudices! You're all against the evolution of the race, the emancipation of women, the right of self-determination, the renewing of the body . . . You always want to let a person take advantage of life only when it's almost past.

CAROLINE. Pamela, you're going too far. Please keep quiet.

WM. BUTLER (*enraptured*). No, no, on the contrary. Completely parapsychological . . .

PAMELA (*who becomes only more beautiful in becoming more vindictive*). By what right do you tell me to keep quiet? My mouth is my own, and, one day youth will bury you all. Youth will conquer the world and you'll be ashamed then that you never knew your own, always living by saving and skimping, just like old used-up candles . . .

JOHN EMERY (*rather amused by this outburst*).   She's got a holy temper, that girl!

PAMELA. In a hundred years, they'll laugh at you. Maybe even before. I was born too soon, I feel it, I'm sure I was born too soon. My ideas, they go galloping 'way in advance of my times. I'll only be understood after my death. (*Sobbing*). It's awful! (*She jumps up and runs up to her room, slamming the door violently*).

JOHN EMERY. If it's not one of 'em, it's the other. Give me somethin' to drink, Caroline.

CAROLINE (*pouring brandy in his glass*).   You do have to wonder where they get all that. When I was young a proper brought-up girl was always modest and didn't even raise her eyes till she was married. Even then she was still almost forced to keep 'em down, with all the young-uns crawling around her feet.

WM. BUTLER (*holding out his glass*).   Don't forget me . . . (*Belches*). Don't forget me . . .

JOHN EMERY (*pushing the bottle away from WM. BUTLER*).   You've soaked up enough already, you ventriloquist!

CAROLINE. Nowadays they don't respect anything. Neither God nor the devil. They know everything, got opinions about everything. You'd never think they'd once lived inside me, or were always hankering for a breast— and what a trouble to break them o' that! Anyway, Dr. Butler, you don't have all such worries!

WM. BUTLER. Don't talk about me, I beg you, Mrs. Rockefeller, don't even mention me, it breaks my heart. When I think what I was once and what I have become!

CAROLINE. You've only got to climb back up the hill, Dr. Butler.

WM. BUTLER (*more and more tearfully*).   It's a mighty long time since there was even a hill in sight. I'm just wandering and scrounging around at the bottom, at the very bottom. And I can tell you, ma'am, that **this bottom,** it's **bottomless!**

CAROLINE.   But if you didn't drink . . .

WM. BUTLER. If I didn't drink, ma'am, I'd drown in a flood of tears, my own tears, all the tears I could weep. When I think how I used to have a fine house, money, good horses, respect and consideration, the most elegant society people of Parkinton for my patients, the most select . . . The men always took off their hats when they met me, and the ladies took off everything . . .

CAROLINE. Doctor Butler!

WM. BUTLER (*doesn't hear her*). I should have been satisfied looking after their hay fever, tending to their styes, and their chicken pox, and their old age pains. I had only to wait—but no, I had to make a direct attack on great sickness!

CAROLINE. We know what you tried to do for humanity. Days and nights passed without sleep, bent over your work in the hope of conquering the terrible scourge. But man isn't infallible, Dr. Butler, and if you failed . . .

WM. BUTLER. Half the region wiped out by my medicine!

JOHN EMERY. Enough, that's enough, you're makin' me sick! I've heard that story more'n three hundred times, and I could tell **you** the rest without a single mistake: the fury of the crowds—or what was left of conscience soaking it all up like a sponge. (*Holds the bottle out to* WM. BUTLER). Here, Doc, drown your tears.

WM. BUTLER (*brightening*). Johnny, you're the very best.

JOHN EMERY (*touched*). O.K., O.K.

A rather long pause. It would seem that, in this confined place, every subject of conversation since the birth of Christ had suddenly been exhausted.

JOHN EMERY. This quiet spell bodes no good.

CAROLINE. What do you mean, John? We're just settin' quiet, that's all; it's peaceful . . .

JOHN EMERY. Peaceful . . . Peace wears me out. When you're peaceful, you've always got to fear the worst. (*A pause*).

WM. BUTLER. Tell me, Mrs. Rockefeller, and meaning no disresepct, but do you still read the future in your crystal ball?

CAROLINE (*blushing*). Oh, Dr. Butler, how did you know?

JOHN EMERY. I'm the one who gave it away.

CAROLINE. You shouldn't have, John you . . .

JOHN EMERY. You got nothin' to fear; the Doc here he's just like my own shadow. (*To* WM. BUTLER). She's been spendin' all her time at it, for more'n a month. Got it bad, she had! I'd stare at her, and I'd stare at the ball, and I'd make alligator eyes at her and spout all kinds o' nonsense in a fishy voice, until you'd think it was more her'n me . . .

CAROLINE. When I'm in a trance . . .

JOHN EMERY. Just between us, Doc, just between us two, I'm not hankerin' to have any trouble with the preacher.

WM. BUTLER. Balls to the preacher!

JOHN EMERY. Well, but you never know. And it does seem sort o' heathen . . .

WM. BUTLER. You are related to the ancient oracle, ma'am, in antiquity . . .

JOHN EMERY. Got to admit on Caroline's part, it gives Pamela somethin' to think about, and excep' for all the jawin', there ain't much laughin' around here.

CAROLINE (*rather hurt*). Of course, for you it's just something to laugh at!

JOHN EMERY.   Well, now, you don't want me to mistake your crystal ball for the Holy Ghost, I s'pose?

CAROLINE.   Just the same, the time I distinctly saw poor Meyerbeer beaten black and blue, and tied up in his burning wagon that they pushed over the cliff—and you heard the news two weeks later!

JOHN EMERY.   Pure coincidence. Just one of those things that happen. Besides, he was a skunk, and a Jew.

WM. BUTLER.   You're just making me all the more curious. (*To* CAROLINE). Would you honour us with a little seance? Just a little one . . .

JOHN EMERY.   Good idea. Go get the ball, Caroline. We'll find out about the weather tomorrow.

CAROLINE (*half unwillingly*).   I . . . I . . .

JOHN EMERY.   Go on now, don't put on airs, you're half dyin' to get at it. Besides, one must always honour the requests of the guests.

CAROLINE.   Well, I will, but . . . you keep your remarks to yourself. You won't be shoutin' nasty words at me like last time?

JOHN EMERY.   Locked up like a prison. (*His hand on his mouth*). My sworn oath! (*He spits. In a low voice to* WM. BUTLER). You get a good laugh outa this—and free, in the bargain! (CAROLINE *takes a large crystal ball out of the cupboard and places it carefully, respectfully, on the table*).

WM. BUTLER.   Oh, what a beauty!

JOHN EMERY.   You didn't forget to rub it with your polishin' paper?

CAROLINE.   Now, Johnny, there you go!

JOHN EMERY.   That's right, I gave my word . . . Wait, I'm going to pull the curtains just in case some old hermit is hangin' around the area. (*He closes the curtains and returns to his seat.* CAROLINE *hunches over the ball. The two men, more impressed than they appear, hold their breath. One could hear a spider walking*).

JOHN EMERY.   Well, d'ya see somethin'?

WM. BUTLER.   You perceive some objects?

JOHN EMERY.   Don't lean over like that, Doc. She'll see your reflection and think it's the devil.

WM. BUTLER.   Sh!

JOHN EMERY.   She has to have time to concentrate.

WM. BUTLER.   Very impressive. (*A pause*).

JOHN EMERY.   We could maybe get up a hand o' poker while waitin'. (CAROLINE *utters a shout suddenly*). JOHN EMERY *and* WM. BUTLER *jump*).

JOHN EMERY.   What? What is it?

CAROLINE (*assuming a voice more and more mediumistic*). The forest . . . I see the forest . . . Trees, more trees, and still more trees . . . Lots and lots o' trees . . . Hundreds o' trees . . .

JOHN EMERY.   Since it's the forest . . .

WM. BUTLER.   Sh!

CAROLINE.   Pines, beeches, maples, sassafras . . . One beaver, two beavers, three beavers . . .

JOHN EMERY (*low voice*).   Four beavers, five beavers, six beavers . . .

WM. BUTLER.   Hush. Johnny!

CAROLINE (*seized with fright*).   Ah! A man jumps down from a branch . . . He's red. All red. With green eyes. A sharp nose. He has a crown o' feathers on his head.

JOHN EMERY
WM. BUTLER.(*together*) Lynx-Eye!

CAROLINE.   Yes, Lynx-Eye.

JOHN EMERY.   Kee-rist!

WM. BUTLER.   I thought that villan was dead? (*He begins to grow visibly pale*).

JOHN EMERY (*now very excited*).   Quiet, Doc.

CAROLINE.   He comes forward, not makin' a sound, with a springy step . . . springy. He's sneerin' and laughin' between his teeth, all yellow from jujube-jujube. He makes insults, very hushy-hushy. He runs his tongue over his lips, all greasy-greasy. Crosswise over his shoulder he's wearin' a big amulet . . .

ALL THREE.   Amulet.

CAROLINE.   His green eyes are shootin' sparks, sparks.

JOHN EMERY.   Don't keep repeatin' your words, Caroline. Makes me jumpy, jumpy.

CAROLINE.   No, it's not an amulet.

WM. BUTLER.   . . .Amulet. (JOHN EMERY *shatters him with a glance*).

CAROLINE.   It's a scalp . . . The tonsure of a jesuit missionary!

JOHN EMERY.   Kee-rist!

CAROLINE.   Ah! Now he yells . . . a silent yell . . . ultra-sonic.

JOHN EMERY.   Ultra-sonic.

CAROLINE.   Hundreds o' men comin' out of the forest, all silent . . . leadin' their horses by the bridle . . . armed with tomahawks . . . poisoned arrows, dipped in prussic acid.

WM. BUTLER.   Prussic!

JOHN EMERY.   Kee-rist!

CAROLINE.   Redskins, Redskins everywhere . . .Redskins and also some whites. Six hundred men and four white men.

JOHN EMERY.   Calder's gang!

CAROLINE.   Yes, Calder's gang.

JOHN EMERY.   Kee-kee-RIST!

WM. BUTLER (*undone*).   I thought all four of them were locked up in jail at Fort Lamaury.

JOHN EMERY.   Keep quiet and don't shake like a polecat—you make the ball move.

WM. BUTLER.   Calder's gang!

CAROLINE.   Some more, and some more all daubed in warpaint, and their teeth all sharp-sharp, comin' down the river in their canoes, made of zebu hide . . .

WM. BUTLER.   Zebu hide.

JOHN EMERY.   Look at 'em close. Are they Mohicans? Apaches?

CAROLINE.   Hurons, Hurons . . . oodles of Hurons . . .

JOHN EMERY.   The dirty dogs!

CAROLINE (*breaking out suddenly*).   Takakakiki! Takakakiki!

JOHN EMERY.   Wh-what?

CAROLINE (*imitating a kind of birdcall*).   Tikiput, tikiput . . . Holala titikikikput!

WM. BUTLER.   That's Huron. I recognise it. She's talking Huron!

JOHN EMERY.   Well, what's she sayin'?

WM. BUTLER.   I don't know, I . . . I don't know Huron. (CAROLINE *stares fixedly*).

JOHN EMERY (*very upset*).   Caroline? (*Shakes her*). Hey Caroline, d'ya hear me?

CAROLINE (*like someone rudely awakened from deep sleep*).   Ah, it's you John! You cut me off!

WM. BUTLER.   You see, you cut her off.

CAROLINE.   Ah, you're here too, Dr. Butler!

JOHN EMERY.   That ball, it's makin' you act completely crazy. What'd you mean there, just a minute ago?

CAROLINE.   Did I say something?

JOHN EMERY.   It's another world! You were shoutin' and mutterin' somethin' in Huron talk, Doc says, enough to give me goose pimples.

CAROLINE (*very tired*).   I don't know, I don't know any longer. I'd better take some herb tea.

JOHN EMERY.   Kee-rist! Looks to me like they're fixin' up a real massacre! Lynx-Eye and Calder's gang. The red hand and the white brain. Looks like Kentucky is turnin' out like Arizona.

WM. BUTLER.   You're not serious, Johnny . . . You don't really believe . . . (*Gestures towards the crystal*).

CAROLINE (*extreme surprise*).   Don't you know Lynx-Eye's been dead for several moons?

JOHN EMERY.   Well, there's been a pile o' dead-uns I've seen brought back to life in the course of my existence . . . All of them in your ball, woman, and busy floutin' the civilized world.

CAROLINE.   Is that so?

JOHN EMERY.   I'd like to know . . . Look in there again, Caroline, but keep calm this time.

CAROLINE.   No, not again, I'm too tired.

JOHN EMERY.   Get hold o' yourself, Caroline, and make an effort. We can't stay like this in suspense!

WM. BUTLER (*trying to reassure himself*).   Maybe it was just the vapours? You won't make me believe in . . .

JOHN EMERY.   Vapours! Either it was just as if I was there myself, or my name ain't John Emery Rockefeller. Come on, just another little peek.

CAROLINE (*coming back to the ball*).   Of course, you had to stop me!

JOHN EMERY.   Well, but talk the mother tongue!

WM. BUTLER (*thinking only about making himself scarce*).   Well, now, I . . . if you'll allow me . . . I think I'll get back home.

JOHN EMERY.   Stay right here, Doc. If you know how to saw off a leg, maybe you also know how to hold a gun? (WM. BUTLER *sits down, rolling his eyes*). Well, Caroline?

CAROLINE. Nothing, I don't see nothing any more. Fog, night on Bald Mountain.

A pause.

WM. BUTLER. Good. Since it's like that . . . (*He slips off the bench*).

JOHN EMERY. Stay there, I tell ya; you make a good conductor of ectoplasm. (*To* Caroline). Still nothing?

CAROLINE. A heart.

JOHN EMERY. A heart?

CAROLINE. A heart flyin' towards an arrow . . .

JOHN EMERY. She pushed the wrong button! (*Scratches his head*).

CAROLINE. Ah, an Injun . . . all alone . . . covered with feathers, riding at a gallop . . . at a triple gallop. He's heading towards our house . . . **Evohe! Evohe!** The earth resounds 'neath the puissant hooves of the stormy quadruped . . . (*Sounds of a horse ridden at full gallop; the two men practically put their ears to the ball*). His mane floats like a flag . . . The feathered one exhorts his steed: faster and faster still he goes! (*The sounds of galloping draw nearer*). His eyes do blaze . . . his breath doth burn . . . Like lightning flash, he slips along . . . He sweeps through space, and hey! over a hedge . . . and hey! over a wall, he flies right through the waterfall, he . . . (*CAROLINE stands up, very straight. Whinnying of a horse very close by. Then the door flies open from a violent kick: a magnificent Indian breaks in upon the Rockefellers*).

JOHN EMERY. Partridge-Eye!

PART.-EYE. How! Palefaces!

JOHN EMERY (*aside to* WM. BUTLER *who has produced a hidden pistol and is brandishing it towards the newcomer*). Put that popgun away, Doc! (*Normal tone*). Partridge-Eye friend! Three times a friend! (*Introducing* WM. BUTLER *to* PARTRIDGE-EYE *who casts a mistrustful glance in his direction*). Doctor Butler, medicine man, heap big medicine man.

PART.-EYE (*to* WM. BUTLER). How, white face!

WM. BUTLER (*ill at ease*). How, red face!

JOHN EMERY (*aside to* WM. BUTLER). Careful how you talk, they're very sensitive. (*Indicating* CAROLINE *who has just come back to her senses*). You know my wife? Still the same one.

CAROLINE. Sir . . . (*The Indian pays no attention*).

JOHN EMERY (*with false joviality*). Come in, Partridge-Eye; don't stay over there, all covered up in your feathers. Welcome to our humble abode!

PART.-EYE (*advancing two steps*). How, oh pioneer!

JOHN EMERY. How yourself!

PART.-EYE. How, Potakiki!

JOHN EMERY. How to thee, oh Mighty Eater of Caribou, Bringer of Lightning and Cocoa!

PART.-EYE. Fruitful be your white words!

JOHN EMERY (*running out of answers*). Fruitful be your coloured words . . . Will you deign to sit down in this easy-chair? (*He pulls the bench*

towards the Indian who sits down with disdainful dignity. To
CAROLINE). You, don't stay here. Injuns don't like women around when
they're talkin'. Do somethin'. Knit. Make like you're not here.
(CAROLINE *turns to her pots and pans. Aloud to* PARTRIDGE-EYE).
Welcome to Your Virility!

PART.-EYE.   Ti polt apkuk, paleface, ti polt apkuk!

JOHN EMERY (*pointing to heaven*).   May the Great Fornicator give you
the same!

PART.-EYE.   Honour and glory, Potakiki!

JOHN EMERY.   Liberté, Egalité, Fraternité. Partridge-Eye! Great
Catcher of Wolves, may I offer you a little snort? (*Filling a glass to the
brim*).

PART.-EYE (*with lively insistence*).   Partridge-Eye no drink firewater.
Firewater eat muscle, firewater burn belly. Rotgut! Rotgut! Firewater kill
manhood. Abacuc! Abacuc! Firewater takes away soul!

JOHN EMERY (*to* WM. BUTLER).   Y'hear that, Doc?

PART.-EYE.   Partridge-Eye no drink firewater! Dakota! Dakota, (*He
makes fierce grimaces*).

JOHN EMERY.   Good, good, don't get all excited and het up if it's agin
your principles. (*Loud, as if the Indian will understand better*). I only mean
your good. Me, us, smoke peacepipe.

WM. BUTLER (*in low voice*).   D'ya think he catches on?

JOHN EMERY (*low voice to* WM. BUTLER).   They're shifty. Ya never
know if they catch on or not.

WM. BUTLER (*trying to ingratiate himself*).   Us friends, old friends, like
brothers, Castor and Pollux, blood brothers . . .

JOHN EMERY (*low voice*).   Button your lip, ya old soak!

PART.-EYE (*to* JOHN EMERY, *pointing towards* WM. BUTLER).
Him, no good, afraid, cowards. White face! Moon calf, smell of skunk.
Poo-ah!

JOHN EMERY (*low voice*).   You'da better kept quiet. (*To* PARTRIDGE-
EYE).   Him, big medicine man, heap big magic, make powerful medicine.
(*Uses words like incantations*). as-pi-rine. Me-than-ol. Per-man-ga-nate.

PART.-EYE (*interested*).   Ga-nate?

JOHN EMERY (*mock seriousness*).   Ga-nate. (*To* WM. BUTLER). Y'got
any aspirin on ya, Doc?

WM. BUTLER (*rummaging in his pockets*).   Nothing but chewing gum!
(*Whinnying of horse. The three men sit on the floor and begin to pass the
peacepipe from one to another*).

JOHN EMERY (*to* PARTRIDGE-EYE).   Now, Partridge-Eye, speak.
You can talk, the walls have no ears. (PARTRIDGE-EYE *remains silent*).
The hens have no teeth.

PART.-EYE.   The fox's tail sweeps away the spider.

JOHN EMERY.   The spider does not chew her paws.

PART.-EYE.   One ostrich egg doesn't make spring.

WM. BUTLER.   Fine spring doesn't make fine bird.

A pause.

PART.-EYE.   When river frozen, fish fly.

JOHN EMERY.   Show me your little sister, and I'll tell you who you are.

WM. BUTLER (*low voice*).   This could keep going quite a while!

PART.-EYE.   When horse sleeps, mosquito gets big.

JOHN EMERY.   A stitch in time saves nine. Poor Richard.

WM. BUTLER (*muttering*).   What a lot of tommyrot! And all this time, Lynx-Eye . . . (PARTRIDGE-EYE *overhears the name Lynx-Eye and straightens up like an arrow. His eyes flash. A fierce grin appears on his face*).

PART.-EYE (*to* WM. BUTLER).   Lynx-Eye! Ha! Lynx-Eye! . . . You, medicine man! Ha! . . . Lynx-Eye! Poo-ah! (*Prances with rage*). coca! Coca! Dakota! Coca!

JOHN EMERY (*imitating* PARTRIDGE-EYE).   Dakota! Coca! (*To* WM. BUTLER).   He can't stand the sight of Lynx-Eye! They've been trying to scalp each other for the last hundred years.

PART.-EYE.   Lynx-Eye! (*Pointing to* WM. BUTLER).   Him, medicine man!

JOHN EMERY.   That's what I told you, Partridge-Eye. Him, great medicine man.

PART.-EYE (*still greatly agitated*).   Lynx-Eye . . . (*He mimes gesture of unearthing a hatchet*).

JOHN EMERY.   Lynx-Eye dug up the war hatchet?

PART.-EYE.   Hah! Hah!

JOHN EMERY.   Well, friends, that tears it! And it proves he was only playin' dead to pull the wool over our eyes, the skunk! Tell me, my friend, what's the strength of the enemy?

PART.-EYE.   Lynx-Eye, Hen-Foot, Clever-Fox . . .

JOHN EMERY.   Clever-Fox too! He succeeded in draggin' Clever-Fox into this?

PART.-EYE.   Hah! Clever-Fox, Eagle-Eye, Hen-Foot, Musk-Rat, Crazy-Horse, Frozen-Ox, Red-Cloud, Hot-Buffalo . . .

JOHN EMERY.   Kee-rist! All the tribes! It's a general uprising!

WM. BUTLER (*more and more like a limp rag*).   That's the last straw!

PART.-EYE.   Hah! Hah! (*Makes gesture of drawing a plus sign in the air*).

JOHN EMERY.   What? What d'ya mean? More? Still more?

PART.-EYE.   Hah! Paleface . . . bang-bang . . . stagecoach. Paleface . . . bang-bang . . . stagecoach . . .

JOHN EMERY.   Calder's gang!

PART.-EYE.   Hah!

WM. BUTLER.   The last of the last straws!!

JOHN EMERY.   Caroline, if we weren't headin' into this trouble, we could set you up in a sideshow at the county fair, as a fortune teller.

CAROLINE.   Well, as for sideshows and fairs . . .

JOHN EMERY.   Calder's gang, you say? All four of 'em? (PARTRIDGE-EYE *shakes his head No, and holds up four fingers and thumb*.) Five? Five of 'em now!

PART.-EYE.   Hah!

W.M. BUTLER.   Just like the Three Musketeers! (PARTRIDGE-EYE *attempts to describe the fifth one with complicated gestures.)*

JOHN EMERY (*interpreting the gestures*).   Big fella?... Well built ... big feet ... sharp eyes ... scar on left cheek ... sharpshooter, Kee-rist, a real rascal! What? He washes his teeth?

PART.-EYE.   Niki. Niki.

JOHN EMERY.   He's playing a mouth-organ? Harmonica? Music?

PART.-EYE.   Hah! Hah! (*More gestures, almost obscene*).

JOHN EMERY.   What's that?... I don't get it ... Buddy-buddy with Lynx-Eye?

PART.-EYE.   Hah!

JOHN EMERY.   Friends, we daren't lose another minute. Gotta go warn 'em in Pancho City right away. (*He has now turned away from the Indian who is making frantic signs of denial*). Warn the sheriff. Get the men to-gether. Round up the women and the cattle. Collect ammunition. Shoot the traitors. Dig trenches. Pile up the wagons.

PART.-EYE.   Niki. Niki. Pancho City... kaput! Nothing! Scorched earth!

JOHN EMERY.   What? Ya must be crazy, friend. Pancho City . . .

PART.-EYE.   Natives, all . . . (*Makes gestures of scalping*). All!

CAROLINE.   It's not possible!

JOHN EMERY.   Quiet, Caroline.

PART.-EYE.   Pancho City, niki, niki. Scorched earth. Natives: smoke! Church: smoke! Pfft!

WM. BUTLER (*lamentably*).   Pfft!

JOHN EMERY.   No, no, I can't believe that. Those men aren't the kind to let themselves be slaughtered like sheep . . . If what you say is true, they must have put up a real fight. (*The Indian does not understand*). Boom, boom, big battle? Hand-to-hand fighting? Clashing blades? Bang, bang! Boom, boom! . . . Yorktown? Agincourt? Big battle?

PART.-EYE.   No battle. Lynx-Eye, Clever-Fox, Frozen-Ox, Hen-foot ...

JOHN EMERY (*with impatience*).   Yeah, I know.

PART.-EYE.   ... come out ... come out ... Palefaces. (*Lays his head on his hand and mimes sleeping and snoring*). All, all. (*Again the gesture of scalping*). Dispatched.

WM. BUTLER.   Dispatched!

JOHN EMERY.   The jackals . . . At night, while they were all snorin' and snoozin'.

PART.-EYE.   Snoozing. Hah! (*Whinnying of horse*). You go, in secret ... Leave, beat it, in secret . . . South, you, south . . . go, leave Wigwam.

JOHN EMERY.   Leave my house? Never!

PART.-EYE.   Snail living without shell better, snail in shell, dead.

JOHN EMERY (*with outraged resolution*).   Never!... When I came here, wasn't no land for farmin', wasn't nothin' but wind. I made it all by my own hands, Partridge-Eye, all by myself: my woman, my kids, my bread, even my own trouble. Everythin'! Leave my house and land? Nosirree. Just as soon leave my own hide.

PART.-EYE. (*doesn't understand*).   Myo-nide?

CAROLINE.   Do you think you're being reasonable, Johnny?

PART.-EYE. (*speaks to* CAROLINE *for the first time*).   South. In secret, south.

WM. BUTLER.   South of here, there's the swamps, the Sioux, the Modocs, the Navahos, the Paiutes, mountains of lava, the Chiricahaus . . . (*He indicates utter exhaustion*).

PART.-EYE.   Chiricahuas, pals, chums.

WM. BUTLER.   Yeah, but **you** go tell 'em!

JOHN EMERY.   No, Partridge-Eye, I can't leave. Besides, I'm too old. If I gotta die now, I'd rather die here among people I know.

WM. BUTLER.   The Seminoles the Guapas . . .

JOHN EMERY (*straightening up*).   Listen, Partridge-Eye, I got an idea . . . You know, you want Lynx-Eye's scalp on your belt?

PART.-EYE.   Hah!!

JOHN EMERY.   Well, now listen! You go jump on your horse and beat it fast as you can to Fort Lamaury. (*Horse whinnies*). When you get there, ask for Colonel Wallace.

PART.-EYE.   Wal-lace?

JOHN EMERY.   Sure, Wallace. (*Pronouncing it slowly*). Wallace . . . like . . . like, lemme see, like ' them drinkin' fountains in Paris!*(*To* CAROLINE) Woman, bring me some paper, pen and ink. (CAROLINE *scurries about to find the required items*. PARTRIDGE-EYE *pulls a plume from his bonnet and offers it to* JOHN EMERY *who accepts it*). Thanks. (*Scratches his head with it*). Only trouble is I don't know how to write . . . Doc, you can make yourself useful for somethin'. Sit down here and write . . . (WM. BUTLER *does so nervously*). And stop shakin' like jelly. Try to write clear. (*Dictating*). 'To Colonel Wallace. Dear Sir: At the time I am writin' this to you, with respect, Pancho City has been erased from the map . . . Period . . . Lynx-Eye who was dead is probably the ringleader . . . ' No, scratch out 'who was dead'. Write 'Lynx-Eye and all the quasi Indian tribes . . . '

WM. BUTLER.   'Quasi'?

JOHN EMERY.   'Quasi . . . are pillaging the region from end to end . . . Period . . . Situation desperate . . . Bring reinforcements immediately . . . '

WM. BUTLER.   You said that already.

JOHN EMERY.   Maybe so, but that's what counts. You know how they are in the Army? They understand but they're slow about it. ' . . . immediately . . . It'll be easy as pie . . . Period . . . Excellent opportunity for you, Colonel, to get promoted to General . . . Period . . . signed: John Emery Rockefeller . . . ' Wait, 'Post-Ternum . . . '

WM. BUTLER.   Scriptum.

JOHN EMERY.   If you think so. 'Share your rewards . . . your rewards . . . with Partridge-Eye'. There! (*With some doubt*). Didya get it all right?

WM. BUTLER.   You want me to read it back to you?

JOHN EMERY.   No, don't waste time. (*Folding the letter and handing it to* PARTRIDGE-EYE). You give that to Colonel Wallace for me. He knows me real good. We fought together.

PART.-EYE.   Hah!

JOHN EMERY.   Colonel Wallace . . . come with soldiers, buccaneers, chaplains, washerwomen . . .

---

*Allusion to the Richard Wallace fountains in Paris.

PART.-EYE (*eyes lighting up*).   Hah! Hah!

JOHN EMERY.   You, kill Lynx-Eye! You, be big chief, Super chief . . .
Control Salt Lake, Ohio, Big Bear, Texas, Jupiter, Santa Fe . . .

PART.-EYE.   Me, apo-plek-tik.

JOHN EMERY.   If you like, my good fellow. Have blankets, alarm clock,
powder, lots of powder, boots, tinware.

PART.-EYE.   Hah! Hah!

JOHN EMERY.   Go on now, scram. And the Lord Keep you! (*Waving*).
Tapakuk, albuplak!

PART.-EYE.   Tapakuk, Potatkiki! (*The Indian salutes in return and disappears. The horse is heard whinnying again, then a furious galloping
which quickly fades away*).

CAROLINE (*throwing herself into her husband's arms*).   Oh, my poor
Johnny!

JOHN EMERY.   Don't bawl, Caroline, won't do no good.

WM. BUTLER.   I should've stayed in Parkinton . . . I could've disguised
myself . . .

CAROLINE.   Johnny, if we die, I'll never survive it.

JOHN EMERY.   Don't talk nonsense. (*She weeps on his shoulder*). Now,
now, get ahold 'o yourself.

CAROLINE.   Oh, Johnny!

JOHN EMERY.   Poor Caroline, there, there . . . I was born a Rockefeller.
This ain't the first time I've grabbed fate by the horns with my bare hands.
Remember when we was in Idaho, at Santa Cruz, during mass. Those
Quitotos came jumpin' down on us just as the priest was at the elevation . . .
Twenty-four of 'em laid flat . . . And then at Gettysburg, when I got me a
wig, just for precaution. That Comanche, he grabs my wigs and scalps me,
but he's standin' there holdin' my wig at arm's-length and he sees my scalp
ain't budged a bit; he falls over stiff! And that time, that time I made them
Litch Brothers crawl, crawl on their bellies, like grubworms . . .

CAROLINE.   You're not still twenty years old, Johnny.

JOHN EMERY.   Maybe, if I lost some piss and vinegar, I'm still pickled
good and tough. It's a tough old nut you've got with you, Caroline, and he's
not ready yet to be gobbled up like an egg. The important thing is not to
lose your cool. (*To* WM. BUTLER, *who already has death in his soul, and
is quietly finishing the bottle of brandy*). Hey, Doc! You think you're
gonna spend the time remaining to you gettin' dead-drunk?

WM. BUTLER (*mostly to himself*).   . . . I could've disguised myself . . .a
false beard, a sailor suit . . . I could've looked for another job, not so
dangerous, where I wouldn't've been concerned with the welfare of
humanity . . .

JOHN EMERY (*has had enough, grabs* WM. BUTLER *by the
collar*).   The welfare of humanity! Right at this minute, humanity is just
us, you included—and it's hard to say, lookin' at you, whether it's worth
the trouble of fightin' to preserve a specimen o' your kind!

WM. BUTLER.   Don't be so hard on me, Johnny!

JOHN EMERY.   I'm not hittin' you, kid, we're all in the same boat. But
startin' right now, since I'm taking command of these operations, you're
my subordinate and you gotta do as I say.

WM. BUTLER.   Yes, Johnny.

JOHN EMERY.   Anyhow, you haven't got much choice. You can either get yourself skinned alive by them savages, or get yourself shot by John Emery Rockefeller if you try to desert. You understand that clearly?

WM. BUTLER.   Yes, Johnny. (*Sighs*).

JOHN EMERY.   Good, then start by standing up straight and givin' me a salute.

WM. BUTLER (*surprised*).   Sa-salute?

CAROLINE.   Johnny!

JOHN EMERY.   Without discipline, we're done for. Stay outa this, Caroline. (WM. BUTLER *finds strength enough to attempt a vague salute*). Not so bad! . . . Now, in step, march! Left, right, left, right, left, right, turn! . . . To the right, right!

CAROLINE.   And what about Tom? He's not there. You'd better go look for him!

JOHN EMERY.   Kee-rist, I was forgettin' Tom! Naturally, he ain't here. He's never here when you need him. (*Knocking at the door*). speak o' the devil! But he don't usually ask permission to come in . . .

CAROLINE.   Well, after the way you talked to him . . .

JOHN EMERY.   Come in then, you blockhead!

CAROLINE *runs to open the door. A young woman is standing there, in rags, barefoot, completely dishevelled. The disorder of her dress only serves to emphasize the physical attributes of the newcomer. She comes into the room in a trance-like state.*

MIRIAM.   My name is Miriam. I'm the only survivor of Pancho City . . . (*She falls exhausted onto the bench*).

JOHN EMERY.   Kee-rist!

MIRIAM.   I was working at the Last Chance saloon. (*Humble*). Yes, I'm a woman of easy virtue . . .

JOHN EMERY.   Right now, don't matter about what kind, just takes guts.

MIRIAM.   They'd just locked up the place . . . I'd gone upstairs with a client, a very nice gentleman with a little moustache.

JOHN EMERY.   Yeah . . .

MIRIAM.   Upstairs . . . in fact, it was a new room. Since I had seniority, I had the right to flowered wallpaper with a pretty doe every so often . . . What was I saying? Ah, yes, I remember: We'd got on to the preliminaries—he was very proper. And I was thinking, now, Miriam, it's the big trip, around the world in eighty days, as my pal Rosie says, she's swell, Portuguese . . . (*While she is speaking,* JOHN EMERY *looks her over thoroughly and appears obviously disturbed*).

JOHN EMERY.   Yeah . . .

MIRIAM.   Why do you have to stare at me like that?

JOHN EMERY.   Oh, nothin', nothin', go ahead.

WM. BUTLER (*greedily putting her back on the track*).   ' . . . around the world in eighty days . . . '

MIRIAM.   Oh, yes! Well, just then my gentleman says to me, very properly he says: 'I'm all washed out birdie. If you don't mind, I'm going to grab forty and charge up the battery.' And just like that, he turns his back and

starts to snore as if I was his little sister . . . Men, nowadays they haven't got
the resistance they used to have.

JOHN EMERY.   Yeah . . .

MIRIAM.   But I couldn't shut an eye. It was like a premonition. An hour
goes by. I feel more and more worried and upset. Just like a premonition,
as if . . . (*She suddenly rises, her face reflecting the memories of the tragic
sight she has just witnessed, and with miraculous inspiration, she begins*).

O terrors never known, o stirring, rustling Alp!
O timepiece in the night whose tick-tock lifts the scalp!
Down from the skies there fell a most delirious calm
Persuading me that now the gods had all gone home!
Sweet slumber, sails all set, had hoisted all its spars;
I heard the breathing sighs of all the trembling stars.
Yet the surrender of soft to Morpheus would not come;
Affrighted as I was, from pleasure didst I roam . . .
The man who honoured me was resting by my side,
Far gone in sleep was he, and fist in mouth didst bide.
How many have I seen: males quick, and then undone,
In milky, foolish sleep, allow themselves to drown!
[The businessman so gruff, upon a woman's breast,
Is like a child once more, resumes his childish quest.]
I could not close an eye; I opened wide my soul
To see the anguish there that kept me thus in thrall.
'Twas in vain. Through the pane what of the sky I'd see
Spoke only of the peace to be or not to be.
O deceitful Nature! which respite cruel bestows,
Even in blaze of noon, o'er us a black tide flows!
About and all 'round me, I hear the shadows stir,
As though a distant chant made echoes sinister.
'Tis not a murm'ring sigh, but lamentation shrill
Not to be mistaken for lovers' cry of thrill.
Half risen from my bed, half dead in a cold sweat,
My frightened body now is not what men covet!
A hurricane of noise sweeps upward in a trice,
Resounding on all sides, it turns my blood to ice.
Pure instinct makes me act, commands my troubled brain:
With one bound, to the floor, and now bent o'er in twain,
I creep beneath the bed, a hiding-place to seek.
The door bursts open wide; the poor man now so meek
Is struck down by the blows of those fierce Comanches
With warbirds painted on their bulging thoraxes.
It's done now; he's no more. Or rather, he makes two:
He's here, his head is there, in a pool of red goo.
But now, oh horrid sight; that ball begins to slide,
To slip, to roll towards me, his temporary bride,
With my own hamds, I must, beneath the lovers' place,
Repulse the leer upon that startled, ghostly face!
The Redskins, satisfied, in whisp'ry, feath'ry hush,

Rush out to other places to smear their bloody brush.
From end to end the city is like a smould'ring bed,
The firmament is flouted with blood and rapine red.
And now behold! the night [the prey of monstrous sires]
Delivers from its womb a sea of flaming pyres.
Pancho! Pancho City! St. Lawrence on his grill!
What crime didst thou commit that thus thou payst the bill?
By these atrocious flares, scarce dimmer than the sum,
I dress myself and flee, much like the 'Amazon
With naked breast,' her hair unknotted and unpinned,
A scene that artists all have dreamed of having limned.
Outside, a fiery wind licks me with greedy lips,
The stench of burning flesh through throat and nostrils rips.
The thorough savages, who struck with lightning's haste,
Behind them nothing left; the city is laid waste!
Mutilated corpses, scattered hither, thither,
Starving babes still hanging at the breast of mother,
Innocents and sinners emit their final squawks,
Their heads split open wide from blows of tomahawks;
My shadow now slips by; it follows me in shame;
I'm harassed on all sides by timbers all aflame.
I leap, I gasp for breath; I think I sometimes hear
Some bits, some shreds of flesh that fly behind my ear.
Not a single wagon nor buggy is in sight
That is not overturned, with arrows full bedight.
Now in a winding street, there stands a half-blind roan;
It stares at me and neighs, falls over with a groan.
A hand up in the air, with fingers stiff that snap,
Flies upward towards a star, then lets go with a slap.
A little farther on, a pack of rodent creatures
Which stare with beady eyes at all of my best features!
I stumble, I cry out, I go on, I can not . . .
I . . . I fall to my knees on entrails still quite hot!
Inside my splitting head, there tolls a fiery bell
To bury gods and men, and sound their fun'ral knell . . .
However, I get up . . .

JOHN EMERY.   . . . enough now, time does press.
Besides, this taste for gore can lead to drunkenness.
You're at home here, my child, with the Rockefellers.
You got nothin' to fear for the time bein'.

MIRIAM.   And if I'm still alive today, and in this room, Accord this miracle to my Celestial Groom! (*She sits down*).

JOHN EMERY.   Yeah, well, you could say it's halfways miraculous. We'll thank the Lord when we have the time. Right now . . .

CAROLINE.   Perhaps you'd like to wash up a bit, miss?

JOHN EMERY.   No more primpin' and fussin' now! It's not the time for that! We're gonna set up our defences and the sooner the better.

PAMELA *appears, pretty as a flower, at the head of the steps. She has spent the time since her exit making up and reading a romantic love story in a comic book.*

PAMELA. Is something happening?

CAROLINE. Can you bear to tear yourself away from your dime novels?

JOHN EMERY. Well, for once you come in at the right time. Go look for Tom and bring him back right away.

PAMELA. But how . . .

JOHN EMERY. Drag him in by his hair, or by whatever you can catch hold of, but make him return to the bosom of his family—pronto!

PAMELA. I don't know where he is!

JOHN EMERGY. Ya must know better than I do.

PAMELA (*looking towards* MIRIAM). But what's going on?

JOHN EMERY. It just happens that we're all gonna get slaughtered unless the devil starts walking on crutches. Just think how them Redskins are dreamin' of strokin' your nice long curls . . . Now, go find Tom, I tell ya!

PAMELA. All right, all right, don't yell! I'm going . . .

CAROLINE. Be careful, Pamela. Mind where you step . . .

PAMELA. Around here? In these boondocks? (*She exits*).

JOHN EMERY (*to* MIRIAM). Now, you, my girl, d'ya know how to shoot?

MIRIAM. Do I know how to shoot! They used to call me 'Little Sure-Shot'.

JOHN EMERY (*dumbfounded*). How's 'at again?

MIRIAM. Little Sure-Shot, they called me.

JOHN EMERY. **You, you're** Little Sure-Shot? Well, now!

CAROLINE. Why, we've heard tell about your shootin' performances!

MIRIAN. I beat Frank Ellington three times with a Colt and . . .

JOHN EMERY. . . . and that scoundrel Bill Cole with a carbine, I know. Providence! The gift of Providence, that's what you are! . . . Without counting the Doc who ain't got guts, that makes five expert marksmen with a firepower of X squared. I wouldn't want to find me facin' myself!

CAROLINE. You're forgetting, Johnny, that maybe there's hundreds of them . . .

JOHN EMERY. Yeah, but disorganized. They shoot each other in the leg with their arrows. And they don't win no battles with their yellin' . . . While waitin' for Colonel Wallace, we're goin' to give 'em a reception from foxy gran'pa they'll never forget! . . . Hey, Doc, instead o' starin' at that gal with them hungry eyes, go get the ammunition boxes in the other room, and the rifles and the extra water buckets in case o' fire—and try to walk straight . . .

WM. BUTLER. Yes, Johnny. (*He exits*).

JOHN EMERY. Go show him, Caroline, I want to say something to the young lady . . .

CAROLINE. Oh, Johnny, you'll always be the same! . . . I'm coming, Dr. Butler! (*She exits*).

JOHN EMERY (*slightly embarrassed*). Tell me, girl, your mother . . . was she maybe called Snow-White?

MIRIAM (*very surprised, speechless for a moment*). Yes, Snow-White. How did you know?

JOHN EMERY. When you came in, it came to me. It's amazin' how much you look like her!

MIRIAM. Oh! That's why you were staring at me! You knew her then?

JOHN EMERY. Well, yeah, pretty well . . .

MIRIAM. She used to work in a textile factory, but then with the depression and being laid off . . .

JOHN EMERY. She was a good-hearted soul . . . And beautiful as you, enough to make St. Joseph lose his religion! One day, maybe twenty years ago, there abouts, she sent me a letter. She said she had just had a baby, a girl . . . (*He scratches his head*) . . . and . . . and . . .

MIRIAM. When I was a kid, she often used to say to me: 'You got no call to be ashamed of your pa. Your pa, now, **he** wasn't just anybody . . .' '

JOHN EMERY (*touched*). She said that, did she? . . . I never answered her. Y'know me, writin' . . . I heard, just by chance, she died a couple of years ago. While you was talkin' just now, I thought I could hear her voice, the same sounds . . .

MIRIAM (*somewhat tight in the throat*). But then, Mr. Rockefeller . . . but then . . . you think that . . .

JOHN EMERY. Just a minute, I don't think nothin'. There's no lack o' coincidences . . . And besides, my girl, I'm goin' to tell you somethin' . . . when there's a little peace on a bit o' this stinkin' earth, you mustn't disturb it. It's sacred, as you might say. Caroline, now, she's the best and most respectable of women, and she's got blind trust in me, absolutely blind . . .

MIRIAM (*heroically*). Oh, I understand, Mr. Rockefeller.

JOHN EMERY (*wiping away a potential tear, and with fierce pride*). Little Sure-Shot! That doesn't surprise me! (WM. BULTER *returns, sweating and puffing, trying to hold onto an armful of rifles*).

WM. BUTLER. If the ladies and gentlemen will help themselves . . .

JOHN EMERY. You remind me of some dope who found some spit in his soup. (*Taking a rifle from him*). Here y'are, Little Sure-Shot, just so your trigger-finger don't get rusty . . . (MIRIAM *with deft movements, opens the breech, making sure the piece is in proper condition*).

CAROLINE (*setting down two large wooden water buckets*). Johnny, I think I saw something moving, at the edge of the clearing. And Tom and Pamela aren't here yet?

JOHN EMERY. Don't get excited, Caroline. I know how them snakes act. They never attack while the sun is this high. They got their way of doin' things and they always stick to it. Right this minute, they must all be sittin' in a circle, tellin' each other jackal stories . . . (*The door flies open and shut, in a flash.* PAMELA *has returned, out of breath*).

CAROLINE. Pamela!

PAMELA. I go along the edge of the road, I . . . take the short-cut, I . . . start into the woods, I see a shadow behind . . . a tree. 'Tom', I call. He doesn't answer . . . I start to go nearer, meaning no harm, I . . . run across a Redskin. He yells . . . something frightful . . . and runs off jumping like a kangaroo . . . Here I am. (*A shot makes everyone start.* WM. BUTLER *has just fired out of the window*).

WM. BUTLER. He won't jump any more . . . There were some leaves trembling, it went off all by itself! (*He himself is trembling like a leaf*).

MIRIAM (*surveying the landscape*).   Gee whiz! You got him! On the first shot!

JOHN EMERY.   Quick! He must be a scout. They're all goin' to be on us. Lock the windows! Little Sure-Shot, watch the corner, Caroline, Pamela, to your places . . . Hey, Doc!

WM. BUTLER (*white as a sheet, legs shaking*).   If you'll allow me . . . (*Stumbling over his rifle, he goes for the brandy on the table*).

JOHN EMERY (*to the others and ignoring WM. BUTLER as hopeless*). Well, let's get busy . . .

While the ROCKEFELLERS *barricade the door and shut the windows, turn the table on its side, bring up the ammunition boxes—all with precision and economy of movement denoting long practice—*WM. BUTLER *sits facing the audience, guzzling away at a bottle. An arrow suddenly embeds itself above the mantel, knocking down a family portrait: a woman with a large bosom.*

CAROLINE.   Momma!

JOHN EMERY (*leaping to the window*).   I'll have the hide o' the last o' the Mohicans, by Rockefeller!

CURTAIN

ACT II

The ROCKEFELLERS *have successfully repulsed the first attacks of the Indians.* TOM *has still not returned.* JOHN EMERY, CAROLINE, *and* PAMELA *armed with rifles, are watching at the shuttered windows.* PAMELA *sometimes turns her face so that one can see the black powder smudges which add to her untamed beauty.*

In the middle of the room, placed on a stool, a large wooden water bucket in which WM. BUTLER, *his sleeves rolled up, from time to time rinses a rag of doubtful colour and nature. At the rise of the curtain, he is standing near the front beside* MIRIAN *who is reclining on a settee or armchair. She has been hit by an arrow. As in a painting of martyrdom of St. Sebastian, we can clearly see the arrow embedded just above the beautiful creature's breast.*

JOHN EMERY goes outside, looks around for a moment, then returns, his rifle in hand.

CAROLINE.   Anything there, Johnny?

JOHN EMERY.   Nothin'. Can't see nothin' now. They have a way of evaporatin'.

CAROLINE.   That won't last long. (MIRIAM *moans*).

WM. BUTLER.   Does it hurt you?

MIRIAM (*weakly*).   It's nothing . . . it's nothing.

WM. BUTLER (*preparing to pull out the arrow*).   Don't make yourself stiff, relax . . . Think of the little birds . . . (*He pulls out the arrow with a quick movement.* MIRIAM *utters a sharp cry*). There, that's done. Damned poisoned arrow! Those skunks, they're vicious. They're not satisfied with ordinary arrows, they always have to go dipping them in something . . . (*He sniffs the arrowhead*). Well, I'll say flatly: it's not curare. If it had been curare, you'd have fallen over stiff without even having time to say ouch.

MIRIAM (*attempting a weak smile*).   Thanks, doctor. How much do I owe you?

WM. BUTLER (*disconcerted*).   Why, don't even think about it! Here you're one of the family.

MIRIAM.   Yes, that's right, one of the family.

JOHN EMERY.   Little Sure-Shot, we owe you more'n we can pay. When I get rich . . .

MIRIAM.   Thank you, Mr. Rockefeller.

CAROLINE.   Without you, miss, I think we'd surely have been done for.

PAMELA.   Oh, Little Sure-Shot, you were swell!

WM. BUTLER.   A remarkable manoeuvre of diversion!

JOHN EMERY.   I'll never forget how she went right out there and started doin' a strip-tease right in front of that band o' savages!

WM. BUTLER.   That shut 'em up in a hurry!

CAROLINE.   They were struck dumb!

PAMELA.   It was silent all the while. At the end, you could've heard a gnat flying.

WM. BUTLER.   Beauty is a powerful weapon!

MIRIAM.   You're all too good . . .

CAROLINE.   Oh, no, miss don't say that. You're the one who . . . why, exposing your body like that to those arrows . . .

MIRIAM.   Well, you know, Mrs. Rockefeller, I'm used to it.

PAMELA.   Just the same, it takes a lot of nerve!

JOHN EMERY.   'Shoot! Go ahead, shoot!' she was yellin' at us over her shoulder. I was just as paralysed as the enemy!

WM. BUTLER.   Beauty is a terrible weapon!

PAMELA.   If I hadn't started shooting . . .

JOHN EMERY.   Yeah, lucky thing you woke us up, Pamela. What a massacre! The first row of 'em, mowed right down without budgin' an inch and still starin' at Little Sure-Shot!

WM. BUTLER.   The second row, same thing.

CAROLINE.   Yes, and then the third row, still dazzled by the celestial vision.

PAMELA.   You'd have thought it was Little Sure-Shot who was firing at them from every pore of her body!

MIRIAM.   You're too good!

JOHN EMERY.   It was only the seventh row that spoiled the show . . . All of a sudden, they were reg'lar cannibals. Shoutin' enough to make the hair stand up on a bald man's head. Little Sure-Shot just had time enough to get back in the house. If she only hadn't caught that damned arrow!

WM. BUTLER.   The arrow of a eunuch—there's no other explanation for it.

PAMELA. It was coming pretty hot for a while, but thanks to you, we had a glorious experience.

JOHN EMERY. A great experience! I don't think you can find such an exceptional feat of arms anywhere in military history.

MIRIAM. You were all exceptional. After I couldn't do anything more, you fought off all the attacks . . .

JOHN EMERY. Have to admit we put up a hell of a fight!

CAROLINE. Even Dr. Butler who showed courage beyond his strength. Always at the danger spot. When he aimed at one, it was always another one that fell down.

JOHN EMERY. It never failed!

WM. BUTLER (*again sniffing at the arrowhead*). Cortisone. I'll bet it's cortisone.

CAROLINE. That's bad, is it?

WM. BUTLER. Well, it's not as bad as curare.

PAMELA. Be careful. I can't see anything, but I hear something. (*Everyone holds his breath*).

CAROLINE. Maybe it's Tom?

JOHN EMERY. That one, if I had him . . . !

WM. BUTLER. Sh! Sh!

Silence.

PAMELA. I must have been dreaming.

MIRIAM. It's my heart pounding . . . I can hear it as if it was a clock . . .

WM. BUTLER. Would you like a little honey and water?

MIRIAM (*highly delirious*). What I'd like is a white horse hitched up to a new gig and a black coachman . . . And on Sundays I'll put on my big hat with the veils, my dress with the long ribbons, my high-heeled slippers; I'll climb into my gig and all morning I'll ride up and down main street . . .

JOHN EMERY. I promise you, that if we ever get outa this hot spot, you'll have your gig, by Rockefeller! (*He spits*).

MIRIAM. Everybody will stop and stare, astonished. They'll say 'Look! Who's that beautiful stranger? Do you know her?—No.—What about you, Mrs. Pickwick?—No.—And you, Mr. Boston?—Not at all, I don't know who it could be . . .' And every Sunday, I'll drive round gaily like that. And every Sunday they'll say: 'Look! Who's that beautiful stranger? Do you know her?'

WM. BUTLER. Don't talk now, miss, you'll make your fever go higher.

MIRIAM. Thank you, Dr. Butler. You are a saint.

WM. BUTLER. A criminal. I'm a criminal.

MIRIAM. Criminal or saint, I don't see any difference.

WM. BUTLER. Please, be quiet now. Don't talk about anything. (*He takes her pulse*). Damned poisoned arrow!

JOHN EMERY. What about Colonel Wallace? Where's he fooling around?

PAMELA. Assuming Partridge-Eye succeeded in reaching him!

JOHN EMERY. You can't find 'em any more clever than Partridge-Eye, or any faster. Like a flash, he is!

PAMELA. I agree.

JOHN EMERY. What d'ya say, Caroline, about puttin' down your gun a little and havin' a go at the ball?

CAROLINE. No, Johnny, I'd never be able to concentrate now. I'm too excited with all this . . .

JOHN EMERY. Just try it a little, Caroline, maybe you can get the current turned on.

CAROLINE. Well, if you insist . . . But really . . . (*She leaves her position, lifts the water bucket from the stool and puts the crystal ball in its place*).

PAMELA. You and your crystal ball, what a world! You'd think we were back in the Middle Ages.

JOHN EMERY. You keep outa this, Pamela. Keep your eyes open. And don't be dreamin' about catbirds. If you spy somethin' movin' or somethin' pretendin' to be still . . .

PAMELA. I promised you if I get out of this alive, I'm leaving for good!

JOHN EMERY. Just remind yourself, my daughter dear, when a person leaves one place, it's only to go some place else.

PAMELA. O.K., you can count on finding me any place else, papa, except here.

JOHN EMERY. Suppose you'da been in your wonderful Pancho City . . .

MIRIAM (*sitting up suddenly, her eyes bulging*). Pancho! Pancho City! St. Lawrence on his grill!

WM. BUTLER (*turning to her*). Lie down, miss, please be reasonable . . . (MIRIAM *obeys. To the others.*). You better be careful what you say, and don't talk so loud.

JOHN EMERY. O.K., Doc, you're right. She's always gotta argue and get me riled up. (*To* CAROLINE, *concentrating on the ball*). Well, Caroline, do you see Lynx-Eye?

CAROLINE. Wait, Johnny!

MIRIAM. Doctor, do you think I'll be able to resume my work?

WM. BUTLER. Of course, of course, my girl, no reason why not. You're young and strong, and have a fine figure . . .(*Takes her pulse again*). Amazing, the fever is still going up . . . If I'd only invented propemidon! I'm sure that someday someone will discover propemidon . . .

CAROLINE (*suddenly coming to life*). Ah! . . . a handsome young man in a frock coat, with a hydrangea in his buttonhole . . .

JOHN EMERY. What?

CAROLINE. . . . and a yound lady on his arm, like a watercolour. (*surprised and delighted*). Why, it's you Johnny, it's us! It's the two of us! We'd just had Pastor Bing's blessing.

JOHN EMERY. Pastor Bing, yeah, I remember. Kee-rist!

CAROLINE. You again, Johnny, with your curled-up moustache.

JOHN EMERY. That wasn't yesterday!

CAROLINE. You're in a large parlour . . . Oh! It's beautiful! There's frills and furbelows and laces and gold tassels everywhere, and china dogs by the fireplaces, and mirrors all over the place! Mirrors in front, behind, on the ceiling . . .

JOHN EMERY (*low, to himself*). On the ceiling! Kee-rist! Must be the cathouse in the Big Foot! No, in Pine Ridge.

CAROLINE. Green velvet armchairs, footstools, rocking chairs ... (*In a kind of ecstasy*). There's women, all naked, moving about, just like in Paradise ... They bring cool drinks and put them on little tables ... Oh, what a pretty one! She's coming towards you, Johnny, she sits on your knees, puts her arms around you ... (*Imitating the apparition's voice*). 'Snow-White, that's my name, Snow-White.'

JOHN EMERY (*reliving the scene*). 'John Emery Rockefeller ... Johnny to the ladies ... '

CAROLINE (*imitating voice*). 'Anybody ever tell you you're real good-looking?'

JOHN EMERY (*suddenly snapping back to reality*). Good. That'll be enough o' that. (*He takes away the crystal ball*).

WM. BUTLER (*disappointed tone*). Pity. It was just getting interesting.

CAROLINE. John! Don't grab the ball away from me like that! (*She rubs her hand across her forehead*). What was I saying?

JOHN EMERY. Doesn't matter. Just babblin', nothin' important.

MIRIAN (*exhalted*). That's my place, there in the golden parlour ... (*To WM. BUTLER*). Good evening, Herr Jacob Schmidt!

WM. BUTLER. Lie down, miss ...

MIRIAM (*with a professional tone*). Will you offer me a Scotch?

WM. BUTLER (*holding out a glass of water*). Yes, but slowly ... slowly ...

MIRIAM (*after drinking*). Ah! Thank you, Herr Jacob Schmidt.

CAROLINE (*to WM. BUTLER indicating MIRIAM*). She's not getting any better?

WM. BUTLER. Not even a drop of quinine!

MIRIAM. Do you think I'm still beautiful?

JOHN EMERY (*approaching her*). You mustn't think about anything, Little Sure-Shot, 'specially the past. You gotta ... as if you was startin' all over again, fresh.

MIRIAM. Yes, papa. I promise you I'll do my best. Thank you, papa.

CAROLINE. She's calling you papa?

JOHN EMERY. Well, you can see very well she's delirious ... And why shouldn't she call me papa if she hasn't any daddy?... Wouldn't bother me none if she called you ma.

CAROLINE. Just the same! We're respectable people.

WM. BUTLER. Maybe not for very long, Mrs. Rockefeller ...

JOHN EMERY (*furious*). Doc, if you hadn't acted brave like General Custer at Little Big Horn, I'd give you a taste o' my fists. I don't like quitters.

PAMELA. Hey! There's a man, alone ...

JOHN EMERY. Take cover! Get ready to let 'im have it! He's gonna have a breeze in his bonnet!

PAMELA (*firing*). Missed!.... A white man! It's a white man! (*She aims again. CAROLINE suddenly throws herself at PAMELA and tries to tear the rifle from her; the shot goes into the air*).

CAROLINE. It's Tom, I'm sure of it. You're crazy, you're shootin' at Tom!

PAMELA. No, it's not Tom. He's taller. He's running over this way! (*Aiming*). I've got him in the sights; lemme go, Ma!

JOHN EMERY. Don't shoot; sometimes they send a messenger.

CAROLINE. She wouldn't hesitate to shoot at Tom!

PAMELA. He's coming, cutting across to the front . . .

JOHN EMERY. Anybody followin'?

PAMELA. Don't see anybody . . . (*Loud knocks at the door*).

JOHN EMERY. Who's there?

MAN'S VOICE. Open the door! (*Everyone remains fixed*).

JOHN EMERY (*pistol in hand*). Open up, Doc. I'll take care o' him . . .
Caroline, d'ya think you're at the movies? Get out o' the way!

MAN'S VOICE. Open up!

CAROLINE (*retreating*). It's not Tom's voice . . .

WM. BUTLER *opens the door. Standing in the doorway is Gary Cooper's double:* CARLOS. *He kicks the door shut as soon as he enters and leans back against it with all his weight, obviously exhausted. The scar of a knife slash is seen on his left cheek.*

JOHN EMERY. Who are you, cowboy of my dreams?

CARLOS. My name is Carlos.

JOHN EMERY. Carlos? Never heard of it. Where d'ya come from?

PAMELA (*with palpitating breast*). Let him get his breath, papa!

JOHN EMERY. Stay outa this, Pamela; this guy doesn't exactly inspire me with confidence.

CARLOS. I come from the mountains.

JOHN EMERY. From the mountains! You travelled that far just to get yourself mixed up in this hornet's nest?

CAROLINE. You didn't meet Tom, by any chance?

CARLOS. I'm a stranger in this region, ma'am.

JOHN EMERY. Yeah, just a little pleasure jaunt . . . You'll permit me to re-lieve you of the enjoyment of this instrument? (*He takes* CARLOS's *pistol from its holster and hands it to* PAMELA). Put that aside, in the lost and found department. (*To* CARLOS). You had a narrow escape; Pamela just about sent you off to the happy huntin' ground.

PAMELA (*troubled*). You kept bouncin' up and down in the sights . . .

CARLOS. Don't apologise, miss. (*The light begins to grow dim.* CARLOS *looks about him, mentally counting those present*). There's only the four of you here?

JOHN EMERY. Sure. Why? Does that surprise you?

WM. BUTLER (*boasting tone*). Four and a half, counting the young lady convalescing here; but there were moments when it seemed like a whole battalion!

JOHN EMERY. With you, we can enlarge the family circle. You arrived at the right time: this is my recruiting office, and Dr. Butler can tell you about it . . .

CARLOS. Doctor Butler! (*Approaching him*). You were practising in Parkinton a few years back?

WM. BUTLER (*growing very pale*). Me at . . . at Parkinton? You're dreaming! . . . You must be confusing me with . . . Dr. Butler, of Parkin-ton . . . A cousin, who was a doctor at Parkinton, yes, a few years ago . . .

Yes, that's it, a distant cousin, very distant . . .

CARLOS. And who resembles you very **distantly**, Dr. Butler. His picture was in all the papers. The police were looking for him and had a price on his head.

WM. BUTLER. However, it seems he wasn't worth very much . . . Among the family, one heard that . . .

JOHN EMERY. Throw in the towel, Doc . . . Now then, son, you didn't come here just to collect a reward. Tell papa about it . . . You were lookin' over the area because you're a butterfly collector, and because the famous lepidoptus volubilis is found around here?

CARLOS (*with a knowing air*). Yes, that's it.

JOHN EMERY. Maybe there's somethin' you don't realize, son . . .

CARLOS (*bursting out*). I realize perfectly well that I'm now in the only house still standing in a twenty-mile circle! The Indians are surrounding you, and except for a miracle, you're done for—and so am I!

CAROLINE. Lord Jesus!

JOHN EMERY. Kee-rist! All the farms, y'say? Even in the direction of the Yellowstone geysers?

CARLOS. There are no more geysers!

WM. BUTLER. You don't say!

JOHN EMERY. The Simplons? The Smiths? The Neuweilers?

CAROLINE. And the Cadillacs? What about the Cadillacs?

CARLOS. Ashes, the Cadillacs! All massacred, women, children, cattle . . .

CAROLINE. But it's inhuman! We have so much trouble trying to raise enough to stay alive, and now . . .

CARLOS. They started by burning down Pancho City, and now, they act as if they're mad-drunk, their fury knows no bounds . . . (*he stifles a cry of pain which does not escape PAMELA*).

PAMELA. You're wounded!

CARLOS. Just a scratch . . . (*He brings his hand to his shoulder, then looks at his blood-spotted fingers*).

CAROLINE. You're losing blood!

JOHN EMERY. Dr. Butler'll take care o' you . . . If you have no objections . . . Caroline, bring the lamp, it's gettin' so dark you can't tell the Christians from the Injuns!

WM. BUTLER. I don't have all my instruments here . . . Let's have a look . . . (*He examines the shoulder wound, bringing Carlos closer to the lamp*).

JOHN EMERY (*in low voice, nudging PAMELA rather forcefully with his elbow*). Hey, Pamela, take a look at that scar; Partridge-Eye described the fifth man o' Calder's gang like that! The man with the mouth organ.

PAMELA. That's no proof; there's more'n one scarred cheek on earth!

JOHN EMERY (*more and more mistrustful*). Yeah . . .

WM. BUTLER (*diagnostically*). A revolver bullet?

CARLOS. Yes, a revolver bullet.

WM. BUTLER. Rather a deep scratch, but we'll have to stop the hemorrhaging.

CAROLINE. I'll boil some water.

JOHN EMERY. So the Injuns are playin' with pistols now, are they, sonny? (*Sudden Indian war cries are heard. Sounds of very fast galloping*). Quick, put out the lamp! Everybody to his post. Fire at will. (*Semi-darkness. The besieged* ROCKEFELLERS *keep up a brisk round of firing*). You, the handsome dark one, stay where you are . . . (*Noise of galloping decreases to silence*).

MIRIAM (*sitting up*). A rifle! Give me a rifle! . . . with a rose on the barrel . . . A rose . . . a rifle . . . (*She rises and takes several steps, collapses and falls into* CARLOS's *arms*).

WM. BUTLER. Stretch her out there. (*He hurries over to help* CARLOS).

MIRIAM. A rose . . . (*The two men lay her in the chair again*).

WM. BUTLER. You must rest, miss. You'll get back in service later . . . (*To* CARLOS). She's delirious . . . a poisoned arrow.

CARLOS (*turning to* JOHN EMERY). You don't think it would be in your interest to give me a weapon?

JOHN EMERY. Precisely. I **don't** think it would be . . . Listen! (*The Indians are returning to the attack. They are now passing back and forth in several groups just outside, uttering frightful cries and whoops*). Fire at will, shoot into the pack!

WM. BUTLER (*firing as rapidly as possible*). The pack moves by so fast, I can't see much . . .

JOHN EMERY. For you, that doesn't matter. On the contrary, it's better. (*Frenzied whinnying of a horse*).

PAMELA. Believe I got one!

A sudden silence, then once again, the pounding hooves and war cries return, testing the nerve of our heroes.

JOHN EMERY. Don't shoot. At this rate, we'll run out of ammunition. (*The Indians appear to break up and deploy in different directions, continuing to shout. Then a fearful calm*). Damn savages!

CARLOS. Don't you see they're just playing with you like a cat with a mouse?

JOHN EMERY. Yeah, it's strange.

CARLOS. I know the Indians. When they know they're stronger, it amuses them to terrorize their enemies before wiping them out.

CAROLINE. What you say is frightful!

MIRIAM (*singing in a flat, shrill voice, enough to produce a shiver, this hymn which she only half remembers*).

Courage, noble people,
Do not lose your will;
Let St. John and St. Peter
Make the storm be still . . .

WM. BUTLER (*to* MIRIAM). No, no, you must be quiet, you . . . (*Another wave of Indians rides by, shouting*).

PAMELA. They're starting up again!

MIRIAM.

It is in ad-ver-si-ty
And in need for-lorn . . .

CARLOS. Shoot, this time; otherwise they'll think you're giving up.
MIRIAM.
> Holding with tena-ci-ty . . . tena-ci-ty . . .
> (*Hesitating*).
> Hope supreme's reborn.
JOHN EMERY. Yeah, maybe you're right . . . Spread out your fire!
MIRIAN (*her piercing voice is heard over the tumult of the firing and the galloping horses*).
> Courage, noble people,
> Heaven spreads its wings;
> If you die in fighting
> You will gain the stars!
> (*Rapid round of firing*).
> If you die in fighting,
> You will gain the stars!
> (*The horde rides away again*).
> If you die in fighting . . .
JOHN EMERY. Be quiet a while, little Sure-Shot, what you're singin' gets on my nerves!
MIRIAM (*in a meek voice*). Yes, papa!
PAMELA. You'd think they left for good that time.

WM. BUTLER *opens a window. An arrow immediately flies in and embeds itself in the wall, knocking down a plate which falls to the floor and breaks.*
PAMELA *fires, but too late, at the agile redskin who has just shot the arrow and fled into the dusk.*

CAROLINE. My flowered plate!
WM. BUTLER. I felt the wind . . .
JOHN EMERY. You couldn't leave the window closed, could ya?
CARLOS (*pulling the arrow from the wall and examining it*). A red arrow!
JOHN EMERY. What's it mean?
CARLOS. Their way of saying they'll be back later, for the best part.
CAROLINE. For the best part?
CARLOS. Yes, uh . . . that they're holding back on the pleasure of slaughtering you until they're good and ready.
PAMELA. You say that as if it didn't concern you!
CARLOS (*distractedly*). Perhaps. Sometimes I feel as if it's not really me here, at all.
JOHN EMERY. Yeah . . .
CARLOS. But I assure you, miss, I too will make a good corpse . . . I think you can light the lamp again.
JOHN EMERY. Light up, Caroline. (*Lights. CARLOS is painfully holding his shoulder, bloodier than ever*).
CAROLINE. Oh, you can't stay like that!
WM. BUTLER. If you'll allow me, I'll dress it temporarily . . . temporarily, Do you have some wood alcohol, Mrs. Rockefeller? (*CARLOS grimaces fiercely*).
CAROLINE. Yes, we're in luck there!

WM. BUTLER. And a piece of old sheet or rag?

CAROLINE. I have all you need, Doctor Butler!

CARLOS. Doctor Butler! I heard that you . . .

WM. BUTLER. If you like, I'll give you the address of a colleague!

CARLOS. O.K., O.K., I'm not asking for your diploma . . .

WM. BUTLER)*examining the wound*). The shirt has got into the wound . . . Miss Pamela, bring some scissors . . . (*to* PAMELA *who is already there with the scissors*). Perfect, cut the shirt just above the wound . . .

PAMELA (*cutting the shirt, and visibly aroused by the virile beauty of the stranger*). I'm not hurting you?

CARLOS. With fairy fingers like yours . . .

WM. BUTLER (*uncorking the can of alcohol that* CAROLINE *has handed him, and sniffing it*). That's your alcohol?

CAROLINE. It's what we put in the lamps!

WM. BUTLER. It'll be all right . . . (*He pulls a greyish handkerchief from his pocket and soaks it with the liquid, applying it to* CARLOS's *shoulder. The latter unsuccessfully attempts to stifle a cry*). It'll cauterize!

MIRIAM (*shouting*). No, no, you're hurting me. Herr Jacob Schmidt! . . . Please, not today . . . no, no, Herr Jacob Schmidt!

WM. BUTLER (*leaving* CARLOS *in* PAMELA'a *charge*). Take care of him, bandage it with some cloth . . . The poison's working faster than I thought. Must be stalinon!

MIRIAM. Don't come near, Herr Jacob Schmidt!

WM. BUTLER. There, there, it's me, Dr. Butler. Lie still . . .

MIRIAM. Ah! It's you . . . I'll be calm, very calm . . . Do you hear? A bird!

JOHN EMERY (*spitting in embarrassment and pity*). Yeah . . .

Heavy silence.

CAROLINE (*in low voice to* WM. BUTLER *who takes* MIRIAM's *pulse*). What now, Dr. Butler?

WM. BUTLER. There's no more hope, Mrs. Rockefeller . . .

JOHN EMERY, *overcome, turns his back to the group and growls in his teeth.* PAMELA *continues to attend to* CARLOS.

MIRIAM. When I was little, I often used to dream that a wren came and made her nest in my mouth . . . I'd breathe only through my nose . . . And I talked, afterwards, I'd talk birdtalk. I talked wren, I talked finch, blackbird, nightingale, warbler.

WM. BUTLER. You mustn't tire yourself, Miss Miriam, don't talk.

MIRIAM. But I'm not tired, Herr Jacob Schmidt; I'm all alone in my bed, all alone . . .

JOHN EMERY. No, you're not all alone, my little nightingale. Here, you're one of the family. Everybody's taking care of you like a mother.

MIRIAM. My mother, I didn't know her very long . . . Right away, I had fathers, lots of fathers, loads of fathers.

JOHN EMERY. Yeah, but in fact, you have only one father . . . As there's only one God.

MIRIAM. God . . . God and me . . . we're not on the same side.

JOHN EMERY. Don't talk foolishness; what do you know about it?

MIRIAM. I know that I'm a bad girl, I've lived a bad life . . . I could never get married in church, not even by the justice of the peace . . . Nobody will want me . . . I'm just a toy, a plaything . . . No honourable man will ask for my hand . . . Never, never! (*She sobs*).

WM. BUTLER (*very serious, close to tears*). Miss Miriam . . .I'm a criminal . . . But if you don't think me unworthy, I have the honour, right here and in these grave circumstances, I have the honour to ask for your hand!

CAROLINE. Doctor Butler!

MIRIAM. You're making fun, you . . . it's not right to make fun of a poor girl . . .

WM. BUTLER. Miss Miriam . . . on my honour and my life . . . Before all that's respectable here, I ask you humbly to accept me as your husband.

MIRIAM. No, no . . . don't

WM. BUTLER. As soon as I saw you, it was like a stroke of lightning.

MIRIAM. Am I dreaming?

WM. BUTLER. No, you're not dreaming, and I beg you to believe me, Miss Miriam . . . For several years I've wandered about like a lost soul, but with you, if you're willing, I think . . .

MIRIAM. Doctor Butler!

WM. BUTLER. Yes, William Butler . . . And it's William who's speaking to you, Miriam. If there was a preacher here, and you accepted, I'd ask him to marry us on the spot.

JOHN EMERY (*advancing with great dignity*). There's no preacher, seein' as he flew off to eternity durin' his sleep. But I, John Emery Rockefeller, I'm still in this world, I'm a Christian and the head of a family, and in a serious case like this, the Lord gives me the right to be his servant; it's a matter of body and soul.

CAROLINE. Yes, Johnny.

MIRIAM. It's true? Dr. Butler, it's true?

WM. BUTLER. Yes, it's all true.

JOHN EMERY. In virtue of which . . . come here, Carlos, even if y'are a bad un; and you too, Pamela, you be the witnesses . . in virtue of which I officiate here and now.

MIRIAM. It's too beautiful . . . too beautiful!

JOHN EMERY (*to* MIRIAM). Straighten up a little. Do you have the strength?

MIRIAM. Oh, yes!

JOHN EMERY. Good. (*To the others*). Help me pull the fort out of the way. (*They pull back the table and place two chairs side by side, as in church*). Now, the bridal couple, you sit there. Join your hands. Very good. You're goin' to answer my questions . . . Doctor Butler, do you take for your wife, Miriam, called Little Sure-Shot?

WM. BUTLER. Yes, I do. And I . . .

JOHN EMERY (*cutting him off*). That's enough . . . Miriam, called Little Sure-Shot, do you take for your husband, William, Dr. Butler?

MIRIAM. Oh, yes!

JOHN EMERY. In virtue of your two respective yesses pronounced in audible and intelligible voice before this company, in virtue of the Lord's grace which descends on me and which I convey to you, from this moment I declare you man and wife, united in flesh and spirit, for better or for worse. Amen.

ALL. Amen. (CAROLINE *weeps.* WM. BULTER *kisses the young bride on the forehead*).

JOHN EMERY (*attempting to be jovial*). Congratulations, Mrs. Butler! Congratulations, Dr. Butler!

MIRIAM (*in ecstasy*). Mrs. Butler! **Mrs.** Butler! **Mrs.** But—(*She collapses and breathes her last. A Pause. No one moves, not daring to believe this terrible reality*).

WM. BUTLER. It's over! (*He closes her eyes*). She died in joy . . .

JOHN EMERY. My sympathy, Dr. Butler . . .

WM. BUTLER. I would have made her my wife, the two of us would have lived in dignity, I . . . (*He weeps*).

JOHN EMERY. I know, Doc; you just came up several degrees in my estimation. You acted just like my son-in-law.

CAROLINE (*weeping*). Poor little dove, poor little one!

JOHN EMERY. Lord, there's times when life and death are separated only by a hair . . . Lord, just as you blessed this quick marriage, I ask you to bless the soul of your servant, Mrs. William Butler, which she has just given up to your hands, and to console the bereaved husband . . . If she sinned a lot, that forces you to pardon her a lot . . . (*He restrains his tears*). Lord, you can't do otherwise than to take her with you right away, on your right hand, or my name isn't John Emery Rockefeller. Amen.

ALL. Amen.

BLACKOUT

As the lights come up again, all is quiet and still. MIRIAM's *body has been removed to the other room—which is cooler. It is night* JOHN EMERY, CAROLINE, PAMELA *and* WM. BUTLER, *rolled up in blankets, are lying here and there, asleep, their rifles within reach. Sonorous snores, varied and intermittent, are produced by* JOHN EMERY. CARLOS *is keeping watch. A soft diffused light—perhaps moonlight?—illuminates his virile and resolute countenance. Occasional night sounds from outside keep him alert.*

PAMELA (*close to* CARLOS, *as though by chance, sits up and in a soft, velvety voice*).   You've lost a lot of blood . . . You're not feeling too tired?

CARLOS (*low voice*).   You should sleep, miss.

PAMELA.   I can't . . . (*A pause*). Besides, the way things are going . . .

CAROLINE (*dreaming*).   Tom! Tom!

PAMELA.   Poor Mama! She can't think of anything but Tom, even in her sleep.

CARLOS.   Is that your brother?

PAMELA.   Yes. He had an argument with Pa and went off, slamming the door, just before the Indians began to arrive . . . It's funny, sometimes I have the feeling there's some connection . .

CARLOS.   I . . . I don't think I understand . . . .

PAMELA.   I don't either, I . . . just sometimes I get the idea that if Tom hadn't got mad at Papa, the Indians would never have attacked us . . . Is that stupid, to say that?

CARLOS.   In the Bible it says that a house divided against itself is sure to perish.

PAMELA.   It does? When I say things like that here, they always make fun of me . . . (*A pause*).

CARLOS.   Your brother is lucky to have a sister like you. (*Pause*). He must be glad to be able to protect you.

PAMELA.   We-e-ell, yes . . . but you know how a family is . . . (*Rather long pause*). Do you hear the wind, in the sassafras branches?

CARLOS.   At least, let's say it's the wind.

PAMELA (*shivering*).   Because . . .

CARLOS.   Because the Indians, especially the Comanches, when they're getting ready to attack, make a kind of whistle between their teeth so you'd swear it was the wind in the sassafras.

PAMELA.   But then we must wake everybody up!

CARLOS.   No, no, don't disturb them. The Indians know time's on their side. They're never in a hurry.

CAROLINE.   Tom!

PAMELA.   Do you think we have a chance?

CARLOS.   Yes, one.

PAMELA (*ironically*). You're an optimist!

CARLOS. One chance in a thousand, miss. Because by this time, if your friend Partridge-Eye was able to reach Fort Lamaury, I'm a Dutchman! Colonel Wallace would already be here with his troops.

PAMELA (*very close to* CARLOS). What's going to become of us?

CARLOS. It's not a matter of becoming, miss. We just have to hang on as we are, in our skins, from minute to minute. (*Loud snoring from* JOHN EMERY).

PAMELA. It seems you don't care whether you live or die!

CARLOS. I'm not anxious to die like a jackal, full of arrows, and have them use my skull for a bowl to drink their kickapoo juice . . . But if you want to know the truth, life doesn't hold very much for me . . .

A pause.

PAMELA. Are you married? (CARLOS *doesn't answer*). You don't want to answer me?

CARLOS. Yes, miss, I was married . . . My wife, Betsy, and my twelve-year-old boy, they were murdered by a band of outlaws when I was three days distant from my house. There was nothing but ashes when I returned.

PAMELA (*shocked*). Excuse me . . . I didn't know . . .

CARLOS. I was the sheriff of Williams City, in Tennessee.

PAMELA. Sheriff! Oh, really! (*She is impressed and embarrassed*). Excuse me . . .

CARLOS. Betsy was always saying to me: 'You and your mania for justice!' Well, she was right: a regular mania.

PAMELA. It's awful! Please excuse me for . . .

CARLOS. You couldn't have known about it. Besides, what does anyone know? We're all ignorant and blind.

PAMELA. You had only one child?

CARLOS. Yes, just one son: he was like me, a little Don Quixote of the Prairie . . . My desire for justice cost them dearly!

PAMELA. Don't talk like that, it's too painful!

CARLOS. Since then, for me, it's all a desert, endless . . . I can only go on wandering . . .

PAMELA. In the middle of Indians and coming here to get yourself killed? . . . Why did you come here?

CARLOS. Why? (*As though to himself*). You take one step after another, straight ahead, like a blind man led on by some notion fixed in your head, and then suddenly light breaks through the darkness and you stop and hold your breath, for fear of walking on your own shadow . . . Ah! now you must excuse **me**, don't pay any attention to what I said . . . (*A pause. He looks outside*). The moon is hidden. I don't like that.

PAMELA. Listen! (*One can distinctly hear croaking sounds*).

CARLOS. It must be the Coyotes . . . When the Coyotes are counting on a big victory, they blow in a little flute. You'd swear it was the croaking of frogs.

PAMELA. It could be frogs, too!

CARLOS. An army of frogs, painted red!

PAMELA. What can we do?

CARLOS. You, you should get some sleep. At this hour, a proper young lady ought to be having nice dreams . . .

PAMELA. . . . proper! (*With an enthusiasm she cannot control*). I don't want to leave you alone!

CARLOS. Thank you, but . . . (*Lightly, as though to hide emotions*). Look, if I wasn't afraid of waking everybody up, I'd play you a little tune! (*He takes a harmonica from his pocket*).

PAMELA (*suddenly terror-struck*). A mouth-organ?

CARLOS. Why? What's the matter?

PAMELA. Nothing, nothing . . .

CARLOS. You don't like a harmonica?

PAMELA. Yes, oh yes . . .

CARLOS (*fondly regarding the instrument*). I've never been without it, since Williams City . . . Bob was crazy about a harmonica, I'd bought if for him.

PAMELA (*trying to gain control of her racing thoughts*). Bob?

CARLOS. My boy.

PAMELA. Oh! yes . . .

CARLOS. Something seems wrong, you're trembling . . . Are you afraid?

PAMELA (*in a flat tone*). Yes, I'm afraid. (CARLOS *approaches her with the evident intent of putting his arm around her to reassure her*). Don't come near me!

CARLOS. But . . .

PAMELA. What's your name?

CARLOS. What do you mean?

PAMELA. It's Carlos something, isn't it?

CARLOS. Carlos Rodriguez Laurenza, if that pleases you. My parents were Spanish.

A short pause.

PAMELA (*gaining some control*). Mr. Laurenza . . .

CARLOS. What's come over you? You're so serious all of a sudden!

PAMELA (*twisting a handkerchief violently*). Oh, I don't know how to say it, but . . . there's no use in play-acting when we're going to die!

CARLOS. Play-acting?

PAMELA. Mr. Laurenza, you're a very fancy talker and you take your part very well.

CARLOS (*dumfounded*). But . . .

PAMELA. Be quiet, please! . . . You're passing yourself off for a man who's suffered terribly, for a lawman, a knight of the wide-open spaces, all with the proper accent and not too many gestures—an excellent production—and I think you must have already seduced a good many naive girls with that story, but with me, it won't work!

CARLOS. What are you talking about?

PAMELA. I'm saying what I know. And what I know Mr. Laurenza, or Mr. Wayne, or Mr. Cooper, what I know is that you belong to Calder's gang!

CARLOS. What! You're going completely out of your head!

PAMELA. Don't try to fool me any longer . . . I don't know why you're here, risking your life among us, or betraying us . . .

CARLOS *(with magnificence, and taking her in his arms)*.   Pamela!

PAMELA *(struggling free)*.   Please , don't touch me! . . . Now, I don't care if I do die, I don't care at all . . . I don't believe anything any more . . . *(She throws herself into his arms)*.

CARLOS *(at a loss for words)*.   Pamela!

PAMELA *(proudly)*.   I'm Miss Rockefeller!

CARLOS.   Pamela! But there's nothing to all you said! *(She is sobbing)*. Pamela, there's no Calder's gang at all any more, I killed Calder!

JOHN EMERY *(emerging from the shadows like a ghost)*.   To kill Calder, sonny, ya gotta get up early.

CARLOS.   That's right, Pop, so I never went to bed the night before!

JOHN EMERY.   Hmph! What'll make me believe . . . ?

CARLOS.   Nothing, not even that! *(He hands JOHN EMERY a shiny object)*.

PAMELA.   The sheriff's star!

JOHN EMERY *(hefting it)*.   Stars like that, you can find 'em by the bucketful in all the five-and-tens.

CAROLINE *(half aroused by the sound of voices)*.   What's going on? Where's Tom?

JOHN EMERY.   Don't bother yourself, Caroline, get your sleep while you have a chance. *(He holds the badge out to CARLOS)*.

CARLOS.   Keep it! You can return it to the Apaches when they decorate me posthumously!

WM. BUTLER *(feeling around half-asleep for his rifle)*.   The Apaches! The Apaches!

JOHN EMERY.   Don't get stirred up, Doc, don't waste your strength!

PAMELA.   Shh! Do you hear? *(Strange rustlings)*.

CARLOS.   In any case, I'll tell you something: they're not going to hold off attacking much longer. I've thought it over carefully, and you've got only one chance of being saved: that's if I can succeed in reaching Fort Lamaury as soon as possible.

JOHN EMERY.   Really! You want to leave us so soon?

CARLOS.   Don't be ridiculous!

JOHN EMERY.   And you think you can succeed when Partridge-Eye didn't make it?

CARLOS.   There's no other way. Do you have a horse?

JOHN EMERY.   There's still two in the stable, but . . .

CARLOS.   We haven't a minute to lose. I'm leaving right away.

CAROLINE.   It's crazy foolishness!

CARLOS *(going towards the door)*.   That's the only reasonable thing we've got left, ma'am! *(To PAMELA)*. Miss Rockefeller, as you see, I continue to play the part. I hope, for the sake of all of you, that the writer of this script has not foolishly foreseen my death beyond that door.

PAMELA *(with a small cry)*.   No, don't go!

JOHN EMERY.   Silence, Pamela. *(To CARLOS)*. Just a second.

CARLOS.   Now what?

JOHN EMERY.   Just a little question . . .

CARLOS.   Quick!

JOHN EMERY.   Calder's gang, how many was there altogether?

CARLOS.   Five.

JOHN EMERY.   Five! And besides Calder, supposed to be dead, how many d'ya say are left?

CARLOS.   There's not one left in this world, Mr. Rockefeller! (*He opens the door*).

BLACKOUT

PAMELA (*she is seen only in a dim light as she sings; the rest of the stage is in total darkness*).

Whoever you are, whoever you are,
A thief, a sheriff, or renegade,
A man too honest, or an outlaw,
Whoever you are, I know very well
I'll always be yours,
I'll always be yours . . .

The moon lights up the clouds,
The wind blows them to the horizon,
But in my heart is your picture
That whispers to me this song:

Whoever you are, whoever you are,
A thief, a sheriff, or renegade,
A man too honest, or an outlaw,
Whoever you are, I know very well,
I'll always be yours . . .

That's all I can say!
That's all I can say!

BLACKOUT

Early morning. Cockcrow. Knocking is heard at the door, then a voice which sounds exactly like that of PARTRIDGE-EYE.

THE VOICE.   Open . . . open quick!

JOHN EMERY (*looking through window*).   I don't believe my eyes. Open up, Caroline. (CAROLINE *opens the door. An Indian appears*).

ALL.   Partridge-Eye!

CAROLINE.   A miracle!

JOHN EMERY.   How, Potakiki!

LYNX-EYE (*for it is no other!*).   How, green faces!

JOHN EMERY.   How, noble warhorse! Flame of our hope! Defender of the pioneer . . . and all the rest! Speak! What's going on? Are you alone? . . . Unbind your enlightening tongue . . .

LYNX-EYE (*arrogantly*).   Quat! Quat!

JOHN EMERY.   Yeah . . .

CAROLINE.   You didn't by any chance meet up with Tom?

JOHN EMERY.   Stay outa the conversation, Caroline. (*To* LYNX-EYE). Welcome to our humble abode, as long as we still have one . . . All to honour to your speed and swiftness. Great devourer of space. (*To the others*). Say it with me . . .

ALL (*together*).   All honour to your speed and swiftness, great devourer of space!

PAMELA.   And Colonel Wallace? Have you seen Colonel Wallace?

LYNX-EYE (*sneering*).   Wallace . . . Buttons . . . buttons . . . buttons . . .

WM. BUTLER.   Good heavens! If he spent all his time just counting the buttons on Colonel Wallace's blouse . . .

LYNX-EYE (*grabbing the brandy jug from* WM. BUTLER *who was about to pay if his respect*).   Firewater. Me first . . . me first . . .

JOHN EMERY (*greatly surprised*).   I thought you hated firewater, Great Red-nose!

LYNX-EYE (*more and more excited*).   Firewater, first . . . Firewater gallop in veins . . . Hop! Hop! Firewater, cha-cha, super-son-ic, cha-cha! Sun in belly! Sun in belly!

JOHN EMERY.   Now looka here, Partridge-Eye . . .

LYNX-EYE (*sudden reaction to name*).   Me not Partridge-Eye. Me, Lynx-Eye!

ALL (*terror-struck*).   Lynx-Eye!

All freeze into a tableau held for several seconds; one would think he was looking at the last frame of a comic strip. LYNX-EYE *dominates the scene with a horrible mute leer on his face. The distant beating of a tom-tom is heard.*

BLACKOUT

When the lights come up again, all are tied up hand and foot, and LYNX-EYE *is pacing back and forth among his prisoners, without uttering a word. At one time or another, he approaches* JOHN EMERY *and twists his nose.* JOHN EMERY *reacts with a yelp. Leaving his victim,* LYNE-EYE *returns to his pacing.*

PAMELA.   Talk about living in the sticks! (*To* JOHN EMERY). 'Paradise on earth,' you said!

CAROLINE.   Pamela, this is no time to fuss at your father!

WM. BUTLER.   He gets on my nerves, that guy, pacing around like that in all those feathers! (LYNX-EYE *shoots a terrible look in his direction*).

CAROLINE.   Please, Mr. Lynx-Eye, have some pity on us! (*A pause.* LYNX-EYE *continues pacing.* JOHN EMERY *stirs fretfully,* WM. BUTLER *seems to be only half-awake after imbibing an undetermined amount of brandy.* PAMELA *breathes heavily and shows agitation*).

JOHN EMERY.   Listen to me a minuted, Lynx-Eye.

LYNX-EYE.   Me no listen palefaces. Palefaces always lie. Hypocrite! Hypocrite!

JOHN EMERY.   Yes, you listen. You lend ear because you Great Ear . . . Because you Big Chief! High Muckety-Muck! Kingfish! Big Punxsutawney! Great Monongahela! Big pile-a-crap! Great Prince! Big Booby! Great . . . Great Tra-la-la! (LYNX-EYE *approaches the wily* JOHN EMERY, *obviously pleased by this flood of praise*).

LYNX-EYE.   Hah! Lynx-Eye! Great tra-la-la!

WM. BUTLER (*echoing*).   Great Tra-la-la!

JOHN EMERY.   My opinion exactly. Listen, Lynx-Eye, you not put all the whites in the same sack.

LYNX-EYE.   Whites not clean, not white. White phony! Whites, white trash!

JOHN EMERY.   Yeah . . . You're right for about ninety-eight percent of 'em, but me, John Emery Rockefeller, I am in the other two percent, and, believe me, a Rockefeller, even at two percent . . .

LYNX-EYE (*with great scorn*).   You, darning needle! You, poor as Job's turkey! You, no gold nuggets, not a penny, nothing!

WM. BUTLER.   It won't do any good, Johnny . . .

LYNX-EYE.   You, talk-talk, talk-talk! Dirt! Horse-apple! Poo-ah! (*Approaching* PAMELA *and staring at her somewhat uneasily*). Titipolt abacuc kawawa virgilik! (*With a strange whistling sound*). Xttllt . . . Xttllt . . .

JOHN EMERY.   Talk clear, don't get ya.

LYNX-EYE.   You, old goat, me not born last rain.

JOHN EMERY.   Yeah, well, I guess so . . .

LYNX-EYE.   Me no touch skin bones old goat, poo-ah! But, potlatch, potlatch!

JOHN EMERY.   I get it! You wanta make an exchange? . . . You make it on some condition?

LYNX-EYE.   Hah! Potlatch!

JOHN EMERY.   What condition? . . . Speak, Great Maker!

LYNX-EYE.   Me take girl old goat in wigwam.

JOHN EMERY.   Pamela! You want . . .

LYNX-EYE.   Pamela: xttllt . . . Pamela: xttllt . . .

JOHN EMERY.   You pig!

PAMELA.   You cur!

CAROLINE.   Oh, Lord!

WM. BUTLER.   Should've expected . . . .

JOHN EMERY.   Never! Ya hear me? Never! I'd rather roast on a slow fire in your rusty pot!

PAMELA.   No, papa, no!

LYNX-EYE.   If me no Pamela, all dispatched, karakiki!

PAMELA.   No, no!

CAROLINE.   Monster! Have you no bowels of compassion?

LYNX-EYE (*pats stomach*).   Hah! Me, bowels!

WM. BUTLER.   Precisely . . .

JOHN EMERY.   You no big chief. You little pimp. (*He spits furiously*).

LYNX-EYE (*also furious*).   Dakota! Katoka! Takoto! Ka! Tokata!

WM. BUTLER (*to* JOHN EMERY).   You shouldn't've said that!

LYNX-EYE.   Lynx-Eye, before palefaces, happy, hunt all time . . . Lynx-Eye take squaw . . . Pigeon-Breast. Lynx-Eye hunt doe, hunt caribou, come back wigwam, find squaw . . . Xttllt with squaw.

WM. BUTLER.   Xttllt!

LYNX-EYE.   Paleface come. Bang! Bang! Kill squaw Lynx-Eye. Hunt Lynx-Eye in forest . . .

JOHN EMERY.   Us Rockefellers, we didn't have nothing to do with it, Lynx-Eye . . .

LYNX-EYE.   Hah! All! All! Me, vengeance. Eye for eye. Belly-button, belly-button!

CAROLINE.   Such base sentiments do you no honour, Mr. Lynx-Eye!

WM. BUTLER.   Eye for eye, that's the Old Testament . . . If you have a look at the New Test—

LYNX-EYE.   Pamela: xttllt!

JOHN EMERY.   If you lay a finger on Pamela, I'd better warn ya right now: Dr. Butler, big medicine man, put spell on Lynx-Eye. Magic . . . You no good, like Abelard! Im-po-tent! Eunuch! Poof.

LYNX-EYE.   Poof?

JOHN EMERY.   Poof. Rubber legs! No starch! And your family jewels, Lynx-Eye, your family jewels, nothin' but two mothballs full o' mothholes! (LYNX-EYE *cast a worried glance towards* WM. BUTLER).

WM. BUTLER.   Right! If I can just manage to cross my fingers . . .

LYNX-EYE (*getting back his confidence*).   No soap! Medicine man tied up, no medicine man! . . . Me take Pamela wigwam. Pamela carry water Lynx-Eye. Pamela plant corn. Cook meat. Pamela clean feathers Lynx-Eye. Pamela xttllt with Lynx-Eye!

PAMELA.   Never, you filthy pig!

LYNX-EYE.   Belly-button, belly-button.

JOHN EMERY.   You dirty Hun! You Tartar! We're in your power now, right enough. But your power stops when we're dead. You hear me? Dead!

LYNX-EYE (*flushing darkly*).   Dakota Kakato! If no Pamela, torture number four hundred ten. All, karakiki . . .

WM. BUTLER.   Four hundred ten, the torture of the wood splinters!

CAROLINE.   Is that bad?

WM. BUTLER.   They make sharp splinters out of sassafras wood and stick them into you and set fire to them.

PAMELA.   It's too horrible! I'd rather . . .

JOHN EMERY.   I'd take on all his tortures all at once rather'n see your honour destroyed by this . . . this person!

WM. BUTLER.   Personally, if I were Pamela . . .

CAROLINE (*severely*).   No, Dr. Butler, you don't have the right to think what you're thinking! (*Protracted shouts and cries from the redskins*).

LYNX-EYE.   Tribes dancing! Restless! Clever-Fox, Frozen-Ox, want cake. Big feast. Jujube. Light fire. (*Greedily*). White skulls, drink kickapoo juice!

JOHN EMERY.   Savages!

LYNX-EYE.   Me calm tribes. You think. When sun suck thumb me come back. If Pamela no say yes . . .

PAMELA (*a raging tigress*).   No!

LYN-EYE.   All, karakiki! (*He leaves. The shouts double in volume, then die away. A frightening silence follows*).

WM. BUTLER.   Well, Johnny, what d'you think? 'When the sun suck thumb,' how much time does that give us?

JOHN EMERY.   'Sun suck thumb' means noon for them. Since it's about five minutes till noon and you can count as well as I can, might's well say we've got only a few minutes left to enjoy the benefits of the world.

WM. BUTLER.   It's not much!

CAROLINE.   And Tom's still not here!

PAMELA (*in a flat voice*).   My dear parents . . .

JOHN EMERY ⎱ (*together*). **Pamela!**
CAROLINE ⎰

PAMELA.   My dear parents . . . I wouldn't want to offend you, but . . . but honour, does it not sometimes, in the brutal light of destiny, does it not sometimes seem ridiculous? And must it not give way to another kind of honour which comes directly from the heart? . . . (*Silence. Deep wrinkles furrow the stubborn visage of* JOHN EMERY). Is it right, is it human, is it honourable that you should be consigned to the Kingdom of Shadows, after such frightful suffering, when a single word from my lips . . .

JOHN EMERY.   No, Pamela, it's no use followin' that tack . . .

PAMELA.   But I must! Is it not right, is it not human, is it not honourable that, through a sacrifice freely consented to, I spare you death, you who have given me life?

CAROLINE (*weeping*).   Well, you know, Pamela, it wasn't planned!

JOHN EMERY.   My little girl, I'd like to hold you in my arms . . . But listen to me carefully: if you want to please the authors of your life one last time, do not betray the Rockefellers; answer barbarity with an unconditional NO! (*Silence. PAMELA bows her head*).

WM. BUTLER.   Personally . . .

JOHN EMERY.   Be quiet, Doc, the sound of your voice is tainted.

WM. BUTLER.   Let me finish, Johnny. Personally, I'm sorry Lynx-Eye didn't include me in his bargain. I swear to you I'd've been glad to sacrifice myself! (*Renewed clamours from the redskins*).

JOHN EMERY.   Only three minutes till the final sacrifice . . . Caroline . . .

CAROLINE.   Johnny . . .

JOHN EMERY.   Caroline, I'd like to confess to you. There's something I'd like to confess here and now before dyin' . . .

A pause.

CAROLINE.   Well?

JOHN EMERY.   Well, Little Sure-Shot . . .

CAROLINE.   Little Sure-Shot?

JOHN EMERY.   The ways of Providence are very strange . . . Little Sure-Shot, she's my daughter!

CAROLINE.   Oh, Lord!

WM. BUTLER.   My wife! You claim that . . .

JOHN EMERY.   Yeah, Doc, your wife. Your wife is my daughter.

PAMELA.   Papa!

JOHN EMERY.   Your half-sister!

CAROLINE.   But how . . .

WM. BUTLER.   You're making yourself out my father-in-law?

JOHN EMERY.   I fell into sin a good many times with her mother. Snow-White was her name. What hips and breasts! And kind, too, Caroline; she wouldn't've wanted to cause you any trouble . . . The chocolates I brought back to you from Pancho City, she sent 'em!

CAROLINE.   Those delicious chocolates . . .

JOHN EMERY.   And that my daughter, that I didn't even know, shoulda come to my house without knowing it, only to die here, it's the finger of God, as you might say; a heavy finger, Caroline . . .

A pause.

CAROLINE.   Johnny?

JOHN EMERY.   Caroline . . .

CAROLINE.   Before I die . . . I must admit something to you, too . . . It will give me peace to tell . . . Johnny, I deceived you, too.

JOHN EMERY (*receiving the blow heroically*).   Ah!

PAMELA.   Mama!

CAROLINE.   There, it's out! (*She emits a deep sigh of relief*). Now, I'm satisfied . . . (*A pause*). You didn't say anything, Johnny. You didn't even ask me who with!

JOHN EMERY   Who with, Caroline?

CAROLINE.   With your friend, Edward Richardson.

JOHN EMERY.   Don't know him!

CAROLINE.   Of course you do! Try a little, Johnny! Richardson, the drug-peddler: cocaine, opium, hemp, marijuana. A good living.

JOHN EMERY.   Maybe so.

CAROLINE.   Such eyes he had . . . such eyes . . .

JOHN EMERY.   Well it's too late now to express any opinion.

CAROLINE.   Do you forgive me, Johnny? (*Strong emotions are felt all around*).

JOHN EMERY.   Women are weak, Caroline. It's men's place to give them strength.

WM. BUTLER (*bursting out*).   But I, what shall I say? A whole population wiped out by my medicine. All my victims waiting in line for me up there, just like in my waiting-room.

CAROLINE (*very understanding*).   Some of them survived, Dr. Butler. Science must be advanced!

WM. BUTLER.   Science! I was thinking mainly of getting rich, Mrs. Rockefeller. You have no idea, when a medicine succeeds, what a fortune there is to be made from the patients! What a wretch I am! A wretch!

JOHN EMERY.   We're all wretched, my friend, seein' as how this world, it's just one long misery!

CAROLINE.   A vale of tears, as the Bible says.

WM. BUTLER.   A hollow of sufferings.

JOHN EMERY.   Walls of thick shadows.

WM. BUTLER.   A hill of moles.

JOHN EMERY.   A perpetual expiation.

CAROLINE.   A desert.

WM. BUTLER.   A germ.

JOHN EMERY.   The crucifixion of artists!

CAROLINE.   And of the best!

PAMELA.   Your litanies are stupid! You can change the world, and give it a different look. If you'd stop looking at the black side of things . . .

CAROLINE.   Pamela!

JOHN EMERY.   My children, now we can only pray to the Lord and ask Him to forgive our sins and receive us into His bosom! . . . All with me, Psalm two hundred twenty-two: 'Closer to Thee, O Lord!'

ALL (*singing together*).
    Closer to Thee, O Lord
    Closer to Thee.
    After the earthly toil,
    Open thy arms . . .

    Forgive, forgive us, Lord,
    All of our sins,
    For it is thy honour,
    And our iniquity . . .

    May we in thy vast heav'n
    All reunited be,
    Flocks of thine Innocence,
    Pastured in Paradise!
    Pastured in Paradise!

Yelling from the Sioux

JOHN EMERY (*speaking, reminding them of the words*).   In the beams of thy heart, renew our faith . . .

ALL (*together, singing*).
>   Closer to Thee, O Lord,
>   Closer to Thee.
>   In the beams of thy heart,
>   Renew our faith.
>
>   The scoffing coyote
>   And the doe at bay
>   All fervently proclaim
>   That Thou art our King.
>
>   May we in thy vast heav'n
>   All reunited be.
>   Flocks of thine Innocence,
>   Pastured in Paradise!
>   Pastured in Paradise!

Renewed yelling from the Sioux. A seemingly endless pause, then finally LYNX-EYE *appears in the doorway and remains there immobile for a few seconds. He is decked out in his finest array.*

PAMELA. Look! Lynx-Eye!

WM. BUTLER. Looks like a scarecrow!

JOHN EMERY (*low voice*). Let's show this devil that Christians know how to die. All together, last verse of two twenty-two, 'May we in thy vast heav'n . . . '

ALL (*together, directed towards* LYNX-EYE *and with accelerated rhythm*).
>   May we in thy vast heav'n
>   All reunited be.
>   Flocks of thine Innocence,
>   Pastured in Paradise!
>   Pastured in Paradise!

LYNX-EYE (*furious, stamping feet*). Konak! Akakave! Potopollt! Me no choirboy! (*To* JOHN EMERY). Me, Pamela: xttllt?

JOHN EMERY (*triumphantly*). You'll get nothin' except by force, you son of a jackal! Pamela says no!

LYNX-EYE (*blanching under his paint*. Kakato! Okaka! Okato!

JOHN EMERY. Pamela and us, Rock of Gibraltar. You can sneak back in your mocassins to the stinkin' wigwam you came from! (*He spits*).

LYNX-EYE. Dakota! Kakato! All, torture four hundred ten. (*Rubbing his hands*). You, old goat, you, four hundred ten two times!

WM .BUTLER. Oh, oh!

PAMELA (*anguished*). No, no! I can't . . . I . . . give up!

JOHN EMERY
CAROLINE   (*together*). **Pamela!**

WM. BUTLER (*with understanding*). Pamela!

LYNX-EYE (*not sure he has understood*). Give up? . . . Tapakikult?

PAMELA (*with a sigh*). Yes, of course . . . yes.

JOHN EMERY. You're not goin' to dishonour us, Pamela! You're not **goin' to let all the neighbours point the finger o' shame at us?**

WM. BUTLER. The neighbours!

CAROLINE. Just the same, Pamela, you're not goin' to throw yourself at the first one who comes along!

LYNX-EYE (*to* PAMELA, *with eyes ever brighter*). Tapakikult?

PAMELA. I just can't stand to see you tortured, when . . .

JOHN EMERY. No, Pamela, take it back!

LYNX-EYE. Tapakikult?

JOHN EMERY. Take it back, daughter, there's precedents. I understand your feelings. In a way, they do your honour. But remember what I always told you, Pamela: it's better to die standin' up than to live on your knees.

WM. BUTLER. Personally . . .

LYNX-EYE. Tapakikult?

PAMELA. I'm the one who'll live on my knees, Papa, to allow you to remain standing.

JOHN EMERY. No, Pamela, standin' or not, I'd die o' shame!

PAMELA. In any case, a woman is always more or less living on her knees.

CAROLINE (*offended*). Now where did you get that, Pamela?

LYNX-EYE (*sparkling*). You, tapakikult?

PAMELA (*bowing her head*). Yes, Lynx-Eye, my mind's made up: tapakikult!

LYNX-EYE (*exultant*). You, xttllt with Lynx-Eye!

PAMELA (*weakly*). Yes. (LYNX-EYE, *now burning up, unties* PAMELA, *dragging her along brutually, throws her on the bed*).

JOHN EMERY. Here! In front of us!

LYNX-EYE. Vengeance! Belly-button, belly-button. (*To* PAMELA). You practise xttllt with Lynx-Eye.

CAROLINE. It's too horrible!

JOHN EMERY. I forbid you to say that word!

LYNX-EYE. Say!

WM. BUTLER. If I could only cross my fingers . . .

LYNX-EYE. Xttllt?

WM. BUTLER. That's it, I've got it!

LYNX-EYE. You, say: xttl . . . (*We will never hear the last sounds of the word. A bullet, in fact, suddenly hits* LYNX-EYE *right in the heart. The fearful Comanche spins around on himself, a beautiful dancing dispaly of his fine feathers, and collapses, struck down, on the floor.* CARLOS, *smoking pistol in hand, is already in the room—no one could say how he got there*).

ALL. Carlos!

CARLOS. Hold on, Colonel Wallace is coming! (*He cuts* JOHN EMERY's *bonds with his knife. To* PAMELA). Quick, help me! (PAMELA *frees* WM. BUTLER, *while* CARLOS *unties* CAROLINE).

WM. BUTLER (*exercising his fingers*). I really am a magician: just when I was crossing my fingers . . .

JOHN EMERY. I can tell you, son, I wasn't countin' on your company any longer!

CAROLINE. How can we thank you, sir? How can we ever repay the debt we now owe you? A lifetime won't be enough!

CARLOS. There's no time now to congratulate ourselves. Get back to your posts. Colonel Wallace insisted on finishing his tea before leaving. In the meantime I'm afraid you'll have some other visitors!

WM. BUTLER.   You'd think it was Grand Central Station the way they're running in and out of here!

JOHN EMERY (*has just fired without warning*).   There's another skunk bitin' the dust!

CARLOS (*greatly annoyed*).   You're crazy! You shouldn't't've fired. Now, they're stirred up!

JOHN EMERY (*continuing to watch greedily for the enemy*).   Got the better o' me. It's itchin' me right down to my toes! (*He fires again*). Another converted! (PAMELA *also aims and fires*). Hurrah, Pamela, right in the balls! (*A great cry of pain is heard*).

CARLOS.   You're completely crazy!

JOHN EMERY.   You haven't suffered like we did, son!

CAROLINE.   If you only knew!

WM. BUTLER.   Look out, there's a whole bunch of 'em! Give it to 'em! (*Firing from all sides, including* CARLOS, *who aims coolly and surely, alongside* PAMELA).

JOHN EMERY.   Hey, Doc, you're aimin' wrong; you're always hittin' mine!

WM. BUTLER.   They look so much alike!

CAROLINE (*firing*).   When I think they were once all babies!

JOHN EMERY.   It's no time to get soft, Caroline . . . In every baby, there's a dictator!

CARLOS.   Look out! I see some coming up with burning torches. Fire! Fire all at once! (*Sustained firing from the defenders*). They want to burn down the house . . .

JOHN EMERY.   Doc, keep a bucket o' water handy and watch where they throw . . .

WM. BUTLER.   You shouldn't't've got 'em excited, Johnny. We could've had a hand of whist while waiting for the colonel.

CAROLINE.   Lord! You'd swear it was Tom, except he's not that dark!

JOHN EMERY.   Shoot, Caroline, shoot!

CAROLINE *doesn't move, as though fascinated by what she sees. An arrow flies into the room,* JOHN EMERY *elbows* CAROLINE *away and fires from her position. Another arrow, and then a third, the latter burning at the end, fly through the window and stick in the opposite wall. Shots from* CARLOS *and* PAMELA.

WM. BUTLER.   A burning arrow!

JOHN EMERY.   Put it out, medicine man!

WM. BUTLER *throws the bucket of water, dousing himself liberally*).   There! That's the way to catch it, cold and hot, both at the same time!

PAMELA.   They're pulling back . . .

JOHN EMERY.   Yeah, a short pause. Rest-stop.

CARLOS.   They're disorganized and paralysed by Lynx-Eye's absence. But it'll be terrible when they come back. How's the ammunition supply?

JOHN EMERY (*scratching his head*).   Well, what d'ya think, Doc?

WM. BUTLER. We're down to our last rounds, Johnny.

CARLOS. My compliments. If Colonel Wallace doesn't get here soon . . .

CAROLINE. He'll get here in time. Colonel Wallace is a gentleman.

CARLOS. A gentleman who likes his tea too well . . . (*A pause. The bitter smile of a hero creeps around his mouth*). Dr. Butler, help me carry Lynx-Eye's body outside where they can see it.

JOHN EMERY (*throwing a glance at the corpse*). I was wonderin' what was smellin' bad like that!

WM. BUTLER (*not anxious to go out*). You think it's really necessary?

CARLOS. When the Indians see their big chief is dead, maybe they won't dare to attack again; they're very superstitious. Pamela, you cover us while we're out. (*The two men carry the body. PAMELA opens the door for them, and holding her rifle, watches the area outside*).

WM. BUTLER (*puffing*). He weighs a ton, this guy. I'm sure he did it on purpose!

CAROLINE (*taking advantage of being alone for a moment with her husband*). How do you feel, Johnny? Your heart?

JOHN EMERY. My heart, light as a feather! Twenty years younger, Caroline!

CAROLINE. Oh! Johnny, that reminds me the Sioux circled us and your friend Richardson, at Grosby. Do you remember?

JOHN EMERY. My friend Richardson?

CAROLINE (*realizing her error*). Yes, well . . . it's an old story . . .

CARLOS (*returning with* WM. BUTLER). And now we can only pray for the time to fly by.

WM. BUTLER. You don't have to. Me, big medicine man, me cross the fingers. (*He does so, and at the very second, the sound of bagpipes is heard*).

PAMELA. You hear?

JOHN EMERY. The Scottish cavalry of Colonel Wallace! (*He dashes to the window; there is a loud yell from the Indians, struck with panic*). The Injuns are scatterin' like eels . . . (*Yells out the window*). Go, get yourselves scalped, ya skunks! Worms! Pimps! (*The pipes are heard from time to time, in more or less loud bursts*).

CAROLINE. Praised be the Lord!

CARLOS. You can well bless him, you've just been acting like kids!

JOHN EMERY. (*acting twenty years younger, as he said*). Maybe so, gran'pa. It just proves there's still life in the blood! In any case, we owe you more'n we can repay . . . You can always consider you have a home here . . . (*Rapid exchange of glances between* PAMELA *and* CARLOS). Right at the moment, I haven't got much to offer you—when I came here, there wasn't nothin' but wind—but when I get rich . . .

CARLOS. Thank you, Mr. Rockefeller.

CAROLINE. But what about Tom? He's still not here!

CARLOS (*light breaks*). Tom·Rockefeller! The fifth one in Calder's gang! (*General consternation, gasps, holding of breath*).

JOHN EMERY. What? What d'ya say?

CAROLINE. It's not possible!

WM. BUTLER. The fifth one in Calder's gang?

CARLOS. Yes ... (*extremely embarrassed* ...). Excuse me, I hadn't made any connection ...

JOHN EMERY (*almost staggering*). You're jokin', hunh? You're jokin'?

CARLOS. I'm not joking. Tom Rockefeller had just joined up with the gang. He was with them in the forest when ...

JOHN EMERY. You shot at Tom?

CAROLINE (*her face white*). You killed my son?

CARLOS (*voice down to a murmur*). I had no choice.

CAROLINE (*crazed*). Murderer! Murderer! (*She throws herself at* CARLOS). Murderer!

WM. BUTLER (*restraining her*). Now, now, calm yourself ...

CARLOS (*crushed*). I had no choice ... (*A short silence; it seems like a century*).

JOHN EMERY (*suddenly much older than his age, in a toneless voice*). There's nothin' more ya can do here, Carlos, that's all I can say ... There's nothin' more ya can do here ...

CAROLINE (*shaken by convulsive sobs*). You killed my son!

CARLOS. Yes ... I can't do anything more here ... (*He cast a final glance at* PAMELA *and gives a tug at his vest*).

CAROLINE. My little Tom.

CARLOS (*to* CAROLINE). I swear I had no choice ... (*He turns his back to them*).

PAMELA (*bursting out*). No, you have no right! You have no right! This man saved our lives and now you throw him out like a criminal!

WM. BUTLER (*between his teeth*). What a situation!

PAMELA. If Tom belonged to Calder's gang, he got what was coming to him!

CAROLINE. Pamela!

CARLOS. Please, miss ...

PAMELA. No, I won't be quiet. If my brother is a gangster, a scoundrel, he's not my brother any more ... My brother is somebody who shares my dignity, my hopes, my honour ... who fights for a just cause, who frees the individual for the greater good of the whole, who gives renewed faith, who enlarges, embraces, who ... disperses the shadows of the shadows ...

CARLOS. Miss ...

PAMELA. That one only is worthy of sharing my bread—or my lack of bread ... You talked awhile ago about living on your knees ...

JOHN EMERY. That's enough, Pamela, enough, you're ravin' (*The door flies open with a slam: everyone is struck dumb.* TOM *stands there*).

TOM. She's right!

ALL. TOM!

CAROLINE. Tom, my little Tom!

TOM (*radiant*). That's right, it's me! Pamela's right and she said it straight!

CARLOS (*rubbing his eyes*). Tom Rockefeller!

TOM. Sorry, Sheriff, you shot straight enough, but I flattened out in front of your bullet!

JOHN EMERY. What's this all about?

TOM (*with self-assurance*). I'll put it straight ... You know, Pa, I always wanted to be sheriff.

JOHN EMERY.   First I ever heard of it!

CAROLINE.   He told me.

TOM.   When I found out Calder's gang was roamin' around here, Tom, I says to myself, you got a chance to prove yourself that you won't come by again in a hurry. You gotta be more clever than the other ones, you're gonna join up with the gang; that way, you can keep your eye on 'em.

CAROLINE.   But, Tom, that coulda been dangerous!

JOHN EMERY.   Let 'im talk.

TOM.   It didn't fail, though; when they saw my fast draw and I gave 'em some samples of my speciality, they took me on the spot!

JOHN EMERY.   Gotta admit you was always a good shot.

TOM.   That's how come I was right up front when Calder and Lynx-Eye got to drinkin' that kickapoo juice from the fresh skull of a big Mormon.

JOHN EMERY.   Filthy bastards!

TOM.   Coming back—there was all five of us—here comes this big jerk who stops right in front of us!

PAMELA.   Tom!

CARLOS.   I had an account to settle with Calder; I came here to kill him. Nothing could've stopped me!

TOM.   Not wantin' to rile you, Sheriff, but the bullet that killed Calder, it wasn't yours.

CARLOS.   What?

TOM.   Otherwise you wouldn't be here to make the girls happy . . .

CARLOS.   You mean it was you who . . .

PAMELA.   You did that, Tom?

TOM.   Right, sis.

CARLOS.   I see now; there **was** something . . .

TOM.   . . . something fishy, seein' as how I was already dead when I shot Calder!

CAROLINE.   It's a regular fairy tale!

CARLOS (*taking* TOM *by the shoulders and looking him straight in the eye*). Good fellow! With a little lead in the head, I'm sure you'll make a fine sheriff! . . . Well, papa, you must have somethin' for him in your pocket.

JOHN EMERY.   In my pocket? (*He digs around in his pockets and pulls out the sheriff's star*). Yeah, that's right. I forgot about it.

CARLOS (*taking the badge and pinning it to* TOM's *shirt*).   Papa claims I bought a whole bucket of them at five-and-ten! But that doesn't matter, this one is yours, Tom; you earned it!

WM. BUTLER.   Fits him like a glove!

TOM (*a bit dizzy with his glory*).   Oh, thanks, Sheriff! Thank you! I'm mighty glad I saved your life!

CARLOS.   To wear my star! . . . It's always hard to give advice, Tom, but you'll see yourself, that star is heavy and mighty cumbersome at times. There's the Law, of course, but there's something even stronger than the Law, inside each one of us, another star that you can' see, and that you're always trying to catch up with.

CAROLINE (*sobbing with emotion*).   It's too beautiful! Too beautiful!

JOHN EMERY (*to* TOM).   Hey, Sheriff junior, there's a little something itchin' me. Now tell me what you were gonna be playin' at while your family's skulls were servin' as goblets for that horsepiss they drink!

TOM (*bored*).   Just so, well, I stand up from that pile o' carcasses and what do I see?

CAROLINE.   What do you see, my little Tom?

TOM.   Lynx-Eye galloping across the prairie at top speed! I don't waste a minute. I jump on Bagatelle . . .

JOHN EMERY.   Since you ran off with Bagatelle!

TOM.   I chase right up behind 'im, I catch 'im and give 'im a pull by the feathers: he falls right down off his horse.

JOHN EMERY.   What're ya talkin' about? Lynx-Eye?

TOM.   Wait!

CAROLINE.   Wait, Johnny . . .

TOM.   I climb off and go over to the body lyin' there still, I turn him over; it was Partridge-Eye!

JOHN EMERY.   The jackpot! You killed Partridge-Eye! That's somethin' to be proud of: confusin' Abel with Cain!

CAROLINE.   Don't scold him, Johnny. You did, too . . .

JOHN EMERY.   Yeah, skip it . . .

TOM.   Then I had an idea: go warn Colonel Wallace. But I was surrounded. The Redskins, it was lousy with 'em everywhere. A real circus, I swear!

JOHN EMERY.   Don't swear, my boy. The main thing is you're alive, and well, and honourable, and surrounded by the affection of your own family. (*The Scottish band is heard drawing closer*).

PAMELA.   Colonel Wallace's troops are coming!

CARLOS.   In perfect ranks and kilts; those fellows can't stand the thought of getting killed unless they're on dress parade!

TOM.   We can have a big celebration!

JOHN EMERY.   No, not exactly . . . There's been a death here . . . Someone who is very dear to us . . .

CAROLINE (*quickly*).   We'll explain it to you later on, my boy, when you're big.

JOHN EMERY.   We must have a Christian funeral. A nice grave with flowers, white flowers, and an ivory cross, and over it an inscription that she can read with joy up in her heaven. 'Here lies Mrs. William Butler.'

TOM (*to* WM. BUTLER, *greatly surprised*).   Mrs.? Didn't know you was married, Doc . . . (WM. BUTLER *is trying to stammer something when— oh wonders!* —MIRIAM *comes out from the other room. She is wrapped in a bedspread and walks as though in her sleep*).

MIRIAM (*very naturally*).   Do you hear the music?

ALL (*except* TOM).   Little Sure-Shot!

JOHN EMERY.   Kee-rist! (*All, except* TOM, *retreat as if seeing a ghost as* MIRIAM *approaches them*).

MIRIAM.   I was sleeping, I think . . . Yes, that's it, I was sleeping very soundly . . . Do you hear the music?

WM. BUTLER (*a sudden revelation*).   Pepetokalt! What an idiot I was! The arrow was poisoned with pepetokalt!

MIRIAM (*delighted*).   Pepetokalt!

WM. BUTLER.   It's a plant related to the families of belladonna, curare, and the small-stamened blue poppy.

CARLOS.   Yes, in fact some tribes, the Coyotes in particular, use that narcotic. The victim is plunged into a very deep slumber. You'd swear it was an eternal sleep.

MIRIAM (*looking at the group with amazement, and singing*).   Angels pure, angels radiant . . .

CAROLINE.   Poor dear, she's still feeling the effects!

WM. BUTLER (*continuing the dialogue with* CARLOS).   Precisely, a true artificial death.

JOHN EMERY.   Filthy bastards!

TOM.   Like to try that, that pepetokalt!

MIRIAM (*approaching* TOM).   Who's the handsome young man?

JOHN EMERY.   This is Tom, my son Tom.

TOM.   At your service!

MIRIAM.   Hello, Tom. You want to come see my flowered wall-paper, with a pretty doe every so often?

TOM (*completely taken in*).   Wouldn't say no . . .

JOHN EMERY.   Leave Tom be, Little Sure-Shot, he's still a minor. Your husband will take care o' you.

MIRIAM.   My husband? (*She breaks into a sad laughter*).

WM. BUTLER.   You recognize me, Miriam? You remember?

MIRIAM.   Herr Jacob Schmidt! Don't wake me up, don't . . . (*Ecstatic*). A bath of blue, a bath of blue . . . It was so beautiful, so . . . Do you hear the music?

JOHN EMERY.   Take her outside with you; maybe the air will stir up her blood.

WM. BUTLER.   Yes, of course. Come, Mrs. Butler . . . Will you take my arm?

MIRIAM.

My body and my mind are all one in a dream.

Oh, do not wake me now, at cost of any scheme.

I am not of this place . . . I ride a snow-white bird

Whose flight goes up, and up, uneven and unheard . . .

WM. BUTLER.   Good. Now lean on me, Mrs. Butler, there . . . We're going to walk softly, very softly . . .

MIRIAM (*allowing herself to be led*).   Do you hear the music? (*They go out slowly*).

CAROLINE.   Oh, Johnny! All the rest of our days, we'll praise the Lord!

JOHN EMERY.   That's right, my old dear; I guess I'm even beginning to believe he exists.

CARLOS.   There's certainly a star shining over your house!

JOHN EMERY.   Sheriff, you'll have to forgive us all that while ago . . .

CARLOS.   Don't even mention it, Mr. Rockefeller.

JOHN EMERY (*scratching his head*).   D'ya still intend to leave?

CARLOS.   I've accomplished my mission. I prefer to take my leave now.

JOHN EMERY.   It's up to you. Do as you wish.

PAMELA.   Life still doesn't interest you very much, Sheriff?
CARLOS.   Well, that is . . .
PAMELA.   That is . . . what if I asked you to let me leave with you?
CARLOS (*lighting up*).   Pamela! (*She throws herself into his arms. They kiss*).
JOHN EMERY.   Nothin' to say to that, Caroline: it's just in the direction of history!
CAROLINE (*with tears in her eyes*).   My children!
PAMELA.   You agree, Papa?
JOHN EMERY (*pleasantly sarcastic*).   Pamela carry water Carlos, Pamela plant corn, cook meat, shine the pots, wash shirt Carlos. Pamela keep house wigwam!
PAMELA (*eyes like stars*).   Oh, yes, papa, yes! (*She again presses her lips to those of the handsome* CARLOS).
TOM.   And she never even wanted to sew on a button for me!
PAMELA (*in* CARLOS's *arms*).   You take one step after another, straight ahead, like a blind man, and then suddenly light breaks through the darkness . . .
CARLOS.   I said that?
PAMELA.   . . . and you hold your breath, for fear of walking on your own shadow.
CARLOS (*carried away by her*).   Pamela, you're a marvellous girl. A true daughter of the West! (*A sudden loud burst of the bagpipes is heard*).
PAMELA.   You hear, Carlos? This time it's not the wind . . .
CARLOS.   . . . in the branches of . . .
PAMELA.   . . . the sassa—(*They hold each other in a very long kiss*).
JOHN EMERY.   Well, come on, Caroline, I got the impression we're few too many here. Let's do the honours o' receivin' Colonel Wallace!
TOM.   They're comin'! They're comin'! They're magnificent! (*Snatching up the crystal ball and playfully mocking his mother*). One kilt! Two kilts!
CAROLINE.   Be careful! You'll break the ball!
TOM (*his eyes suddenly growing very big while looking at the ball, and with a great shout*).   Ah! A black river!
JOHN EMERY.   A black river?
TOM.   A black river right under our feet . . . A river of black blood . . .
JOHN EMERY.   It's **oil**!
CAROLINE (*looking at the ball*).   One well, two wells, three wells . . .
JOHN EMERY (*also at the ball*).   Four hundred wells, five hundred wells, six hundred wells . . .
TOM.   A thousand wells! Two thousand wells! . . .
JOHN EMERY }
CAROLINE   } (*together*).   Three thousand wells, six thousand wells, nine thousand wells, twelve thousand wells, fifteen thousand wells . . .

The curtain falls on this Biblical enumeration, while the lovers are still lost in their embrace, and now very close at hand, the bagpipes burst out once more, both strident and quite erotic.